Natu

D1628324

BARBARA EHRENREICH is the author of over twenty books, including the bestselling *Smile or Die* and *Nickel and Dimed*. She has written for *Time*, *Harper's*, the *New York Times Magazine* and various British newspapers including *The Times* and the *Guardian*. She has a PhD in cellular immunology from Rockefeller University and writes frequently about health care and medical science. She lives in Virginia, USA.

'Anarchic, funny and fizzling with the joy of living' *Sunday Herald*

'Ehrenreich is irreplaceable to the culture, with her rigor and skepticism, her allergy to comforting illusions . . . [Ehrenreich] sits in contemplation of death itself in the book's concluding, very beautiful passages, bringing to it her characteristic curiosity and awe at the natural world' *New York Times*

'One of our great iconoclasts, lucid, thought-provoking and instructive' *Guardian*

'[A] polemical, wry, hilarious and affecting series of counterintuitive essays by one of the most original and unexpected thinkers around . . . This is a book itself teeming with ideas and possibilities: maddening, stimulating, exciting and surprising, testifying in its own way to the expanding prospects of ideas that turn topsy-turvy, every-which-way as we try to make sense of the great unknowns' Marina Vaizey, *Arts Desk*

'Ehrenreich's sharp and fearless take on mortality privileges joy over juice fasts and argues that, regardless of how many hours we spend in   lemic, *Natural   aper is

C334351240

considerably less grim than a life spent in terror of a fate that awaits us all' Matthew Desmond, Pulitzer Prize-winning and *New York Times* bestselling author of *Evicted: Poverty and Profit in the American City*

'Imagine Sherlock Holmes, spyglass in hand, uncovering the crimes of our very own immune cells, as they sometimes welcome disease into our aging bodies instead of protecting us against it, and you have our own brilliant Barbara Ehrenreich, PhD in microbiology, at work uncovering a scientific mystery. Then imagine Ehrenreich, with a knowing laugh and glass of champagne, exploring the cultural mystery of the moral responsibility earnest American gym-goers express – and the illusion of control we anxiously seek – as we step, pedal and press our way to fitness. Then imagine a large-spirited Barbara deeply appreciative of humans and all forms of life, and you get a glimpse into this provocative, informative, hilarious, and deeply moving book. A must-read' Arlie Hochschild, *New York Times* bestselling author of *Strangers in Their Own Land: Anger and Mourning on the American Right*

'Barbara Ehrenreich is a singular voice of sanity amid our national obsession with wellness and longevity. She is deeply well-informed about contemporary medical practices and their shortcomings, but she wears her learning lightly. *Natural Causes* is a delightful as well as an enlightening read. No one who cares about living (or dying) well can afford to miss it' Jackson Lears, Editor in Chief of the *Raritan Quarterly Review*

'Give me a lever and a place to stand and I will move the earth, promised Archimedes. In *Natural Causes*, Barbara Ehrenreich has achieved an Archimedean feat. Her lever is made of erudition, acuity, and irreverence; her place to stand is the perspective of cultural criticism; and she has turned the current understanding of body and self upon its head. To read this book is a relief: at last, what needed to be said!' Jessica Riskin, author of *Science in the Age of Sensibility: The Sentimental Empiricists of the French Enlightenment*

Natural
Causes

Life, Death
and the Illusion
of Control

Barbara Ehrenreich

GRANTA

Granta Publications, 12 Addison Avenue, London W11 4QR

First published in Great Britain by Granta Books, 2018
This paperback edition published by Granta Books, 2019

First published in the United States by Twelve, an imprint of
Grand Central Publishing, Hachette Book Group, Inc., New York, in 2018

A CIP catalogue record for this book is available from the British Library.

10 9 8 7 6 5 4 3 2 1

ISBN 978 1 78378 242 0 (paperback)
eISBN 978 1 78378 243 7 (ebook)

Offset by Patty Rennie

Printed and bound by CPI Group (UK) Ltd,
Croydon, CR0 4YY

www.granta.com

CONTENTS

INTRODUCTION

As a teenager, I aspired to be a scientist, but too many things happened to distract me from that goal, so I became instead a science appreciator. I am not willing to spend my life in a laboratory or observatory, patiently recording measurements, but I am eager to read the reports of those who do, whether the subject is astronomy or biochemistry, and I generally consume those reports in pre-masticated forms, like *Discover* or *Scientific American*. Ten years ago, in the latter magazine, I found something so deeply upsetting that I could only think, *This changes everything*.

The article, written by one of *Scientific American*'s editors,[1] reported that the immune system actually abets the growth and spread of tumors, which is like saying that the fire department is indeed staffed by arsonists. We all know that the function of the immune system is to protect us, most commonly from bacteria and viruses, so its expected response to cancer should be a concerted and militant defense. As a graduate student, I had worked in two different laboratories dedicated to elucidating the defenses mounted by the immune system, and had come to think of it as a magical and for the most part invisible protective cloak. I could walk through the valley of the shadow of death, so to speak, or expose myself to deadly microbes, and know no evil, because my immune cells and antibodies would keep me from harm. But here they were—going over to the other side.

I half hoped that the accusations against the immune system would be refuted in a few years and end up in the dustbin of "irreproducible results." But they persisted and are today openly acknowledged by the relevant specialists, though not without a certain queasiness, indicated by the frequent use of the word "paradoxical." This is not the kind of word that one expects to find in the scientific literature, which is what I had moved on to from the popular magazines. In science, if something appears to be a "paradox," then you have a lot more work to do until you solve it—or, of course, abandon some of your original assumptions and search for a new paradigm.

The paradox of the immune system and cancer is not just a scientific puzzle; it has deep moral reverberations. We know that the immune system is supposed to be "good," and in the popular health literature we are urged to take measures to strengthen it. Cancer patients in particular are exhorted to think "positive thoughts," on the unproven theory that the immune system is the channel of communication between one's conscious mind and one's evidently unconscious body. But if the immune system can actually enable the growth and spread of cancer, nothing may be worse for the patient than a stronger one. He or she would be better advised to suppress it, with, say, immunosuppressive drugs or perhaps "negative thoughts."

In the ideal world imagined by mid-twentieth-century biologists, the immune system constantly monitored the cells it encountered, pouncing on and destroying any aberrant ones. This monitoring work, called immunosurveillance, supposedly guaranteed that the body would be kept clear of intruders, or any kind of suspicious characters, cancer cells included. But as the century came to a close, it became increasingly evident that the immune system was not only giving cancer cells a pass and figuratively waving them through the checkpoints. Perversely and against all biological reason, it was aiding them to spread and establish new tumors throughout the body.

I took this personally. For one thing, I had been diagnosed with breast cancer in 2000, and this is one of the many types of cancer that has been found to be enabled by the immune system. Mine had only spread to a lymph node at the time of its discovery, but from there it was poised to strike out to, "God forbid"—as the doctors always piously put it—the liver or bones. My other personal connection had to do with the kind of immune cells that have turned out to do the enabling of cancer's spread; these are called macrophages, meaning "big eaters."

As it happens, I know more about macrophages than I do about any other human cell type, which is not to say I know very much. But for a variety of reasons, I had ended up doing my graduate research on macrophages, and not because of their involvement in cancer, which was completely unsuspected at the time. Macrophages are considered the "frontline defenders" in the body's unending struggle against microbial invaders. They are large, relative to many other body cells, they kill microbes by eating them, and they are usually ravenous. I cultured macrophages in glass flasks, studied them through a microscope, labeled particles within them with radioactive markers, and generally did all the things a grad student could do to understand these tiny life forms. I thought they were my friends.

In the meantime I had gone on to study and report on events at a far vaster scale—whole human bodies and, beyond them, societies. As an amateur sociologist, I had seen the health care system in my own country grow from a "cottage industry" to a three-trillion-dollar-a-year enterprise—employing millions, dominating neighborhoods and even skylines, setting off political fights over who should pay for it, and dooming politicians who choose the wrong answer. And what does this enterprise have to offer those who are not actually employed by it? Longevity is promised, among other things including freedom from disability, safe childbirth, and healthy babies. In a word, it offers us control—not control over our government or social milieu, but over our own bodies.

The more ambitious among us seek to control the people around them, their employees, for example, and subordinates in general. But even the most unassuming and humble of us is expected to want to control what lies within the perimeter of our own skin. We avidly seek to control our weight and shape through diet and exercise and, if all else fails, surgical intervention. The entire penumbra of thoughts and emotions that originates in our physical bodies also demands attention and manipulation. We are told since childhood to control our emotions and are offered dozens of algorithms for doing so as we grow older, from meditation to psychotherapy. At older ages, we are urged to preserve our intellects by playing mentally challenging games like Lumosity and Sudoku. There is nothing about ourselves that is not potentially subject to our control.

So pervasive is the insistence on control that we may feel that we can legitimately seek homeopathic doses of its opposite—a fling with a stranger, a drunken night on the town, a riotous celebration of the home team. The wealthiest and most powerful of us can sample a brush with the out-of-control in the form of an "adventure vacation" located in an exotic setting and featuring hazardous activities, like mountain climbing or skydiving. When the vacation is over they can return to their regimens of self-mastery and control.

But no matter how much effort we expend, not everything is potentially within our control, not even our own bodies and minds. This to me is the first lesson of the macrophages that perversely promote lethal cancers. The body—or, to use more cutting-edge language, the "mindbody"—is not a smooth-running machine in which each part obediently performs its tasks for the benefit of the common good. It is at best a confederation of parts—cells, tissues, even thought patterns—that may seek to advance their own agendas, whether or not they are destructive of the whole. What, after all, is cancer, other than a cellular rebellion against the entire organism? Even such seemingly benign conditions as pregnancy are turning out to be driven by competition and conflict on a very small scale.

I know that in an era where both conventional medicine and the woolliest "alternatives" hold out the goal of self-mastery, or at least the promise that we can prolong our lives and improve our health by carefully monitoring our lifestyles, many people will find this perspective disappointing, even defeatist. What is the point of minutely calibrating one's diet and time spent on the treadmill when you could be vanquished entirely by a few rogue cells within your own body?

But that is only the first lesson of the treasonous macrophages that inspired this book, and the story does not end there. It turns out that many cells within the body are capable of what biologists have come to call "cellular decision making." Certain cells can "decide" where to go and what to do next without any instructions from a central authority, almost as if they possessed "free will." A similar freedom, as we shall see, extends to many bits of matter that are normally considered nonliving, like viruses and even atoms.

Things I had been taught to believe are inert, passive, or merely insignificant—like individual cells—are in fact capable of making choices, including very bad ones. It's not going too far to say that the natural world, as we are coming to understand it, pulses with something like "life." And as I will conclude, this insight should inform the way we think, not only about our lives, but about death and how we die.

This book cannot be summarized in a sentence or two, but here is a rough road map to what follows: The first half is devoted to describing the quest for control as it is acted out through medical care, "lifestyle" adjustments in the areas of exercise and diet, and a nebulous but ever-growing "wellness" industry that embraces both body and mind. All of these forms of intervention invite questions about the limits of human control, which leads us into the realm of biology—what lies within the body and whether its various parts and elements are even susceptible to conscious human control. Do they form a harmonious whole or are they engaged in perpetual conflict?

I present the emerging scientific case for a dystopian view of the body—not as a well-ordered machine, but as a site of ongoing conflict at the cellular level, which ends, at least in all the cases we know of, in death. Finally, at the end of this book, if not at the end of our individual lives, we are left with the inevitable question of "What am I?", or you, for that matter. What is the "self" if it is not rooted in a harmonious body, and what do we need it for anyway?

Here you will find no "how-to" advice, no tips about how to extend your life, upgrade your diet and exercise regimen, or fine-tune your attitude in a more healthful direction. If anything, I hope this book will encourage you to rethink the project of personal control over your body and mind. We would all like to live longer and healthier lives; the question is how much of our lives should be devoted to this project, when we all, or at least most of us, have other, often more consequential things to do. Soldiers seek physical fitness, but are prepared to die in battle. Health workers risk their own lives to save others in famines and epidemics. Good Samaritans throw their bodies between assailants and their intended victims.

You can think of death bitterly or with resignation, as a tragic interruption of your life, and take every possible measure to postpone it. Or, more realistically, you can think of life as an interruption of an eternity of personal nonexistence, and seize it as a brief opportunity to observe and interact with the living, ever-surprising world around us.

Natural Causes

CHAPTER ONE

Midlife Revolt

In the last few years I have given up on the many medical measures—cancer screenings, annual exams, Pap smears, for example—expected of a responsible person with health insurance. This was not based on any suicidal impulse. It was barely even a decision, more like an accumulation of micro-decisions: to stay at my desk and meet a deadline or show up at the primary care office and submit to the latest test to gauge my biological sustainability; to spend the afternoon in the faux-cozy corporate environment of a medical facility or go for a walk. At first I criticized myself as a slacker and procrastinator, falling behind on the simple, obvious stuff that could prolong my life. After all, this is the great promise of modern scientific medicine: You do not have to get sick and die (at least not for a while), because problems can be detected "early" when they are readily treatable. Better to catch a tumor when it's the size of an olive than that of a cantaloupe.

I knew I was going against my own long-standing bias in favor of preventive medical care as opposed to expensive and invasive high-tech curative interventions. What could be more ridiculous than an inner-city hospital that offers a hyperbaric chamber but cannot bestir itself to get out in the neighborhood and test for lead poisoning? From a public health perspective, as well as a personal one, it makes far more sense to screen for preventable problems than to invest huge resources in the treatment of the very ill.

I also understood that I was going against the grain for my particular demographic. Most of my educated, middle-class friends had begun to double down on their health-related efforts at the onset of middle age, if not earlier. They undertook exercise or yoga regimens; they filled their calendars with upcoming medical tests and exams; they boasted about their "good" and "bad" cholesterol counts, their heart rates and blood pressure. Mostly they understood the task of aging to be self-denial, especially in the realm of diet, where one medical fad, one study or another, condemned fat and meat, carbs, gluten, dairy, or all animal-derived products. In the health-conscious mind-set that has prevailed among the world's affluent people for about four decades now, health is indistinguishable from virtue, tasty foods are "sinfully delicious," while healthful foods may taste good enough to be advertised as "guilt-free." Those seeking to compensate for a lapse undertake punitive measures like fasts, purges, or diets composed of different juices carefully sequenced throughout the day.

I had a different reaction to aging: I gradually came to realize that I was *old enough to die*, by which I am not suggesting that each of us bears an expiration date. There is of course no fixed age at which a person ceases to be worthy of further medical investment, whether aimed at prevention or cure. The military judges that a person is old enough to die—to put him- or herself in the line of fire—at age eighteen. At the other end of life, many remain world leaders in their seventies or even older, without anyone questioning their need for lavish continuing testing and care. Zimbabwe's president, Robert Mugabe, who is ninety-two, and has undergone multiple treatments for prostate cancer. If we go by newspaper obituaries, however, we notice that there is an age at which death no longer requires much explanation. Although there is no general editorial rule on these matters, it is usually sufficient when the deceased is in their seventies or older for the obituary writer to invoke "natural causes." It is sad when anyone dies, but no one can consider the death of a septuagenarian "tragic," and there will be no demand for an investigation.

Once I realized I was old enough to die, I decided that I was also old enough not to incur any more suffering, annoyance, or boredom in the pursuit of a longer life. I eat well, meaning I choose foods that taste good and that will stave off hunger for as long as possible, like protein, fiber, and fats. I exercise—not because it will make me live longer but because it feels good when I do. As for medical care: I will seek help for an urgent problem, but I am no longer interested in looking for problems that remain undetectable to me. Ideally, the determination of when one is old enough to die should be a personal decision, based on a judgment of the likely benefits, if any, of medical care and—just as important at a certain age—how we choose to spend the time that remains to us.

As it happens, I had always questioned whatever procedures the health care providers recommended; in fact, I am part of a generation of women who insisted on their right to raise questions without having the word "uncooperative," or worse, written into their medical records. So when a few years ago my primary care physician told me that I needed a bone density scan, I of course asked him why: What could be done if the result was positive and my bones were found to be hollowed out by age? Fortunately, he replied, there was now a drug for that. I told him I was aware of the drug, both from its full-page magazine ads as well as from articles in the media questioning its safety and efficacy. Think of the alternative, he said, which might well be, say, a hip fracture, followed by a rapid descent to the nursing home. So I grudgingly conceded that undergoing the test, which is noninvasive and covered by my insurance, might be preferable to immobility and institutionalization.

The result was a diagnosis of "osteopenia," or thinning of the bones, a condition that might have been alarming if I hadn't found out that it is shared by nearly all women over the age of thirty-five. Osteopenia is, in other words, not a disease but a normal feature of aging. A little further research, all into readily available sources, revealed that routine bone scanning had been heavily promoted and even subsidized by the drug's manufacturer.[1] Worse, the favored medication at the time of my diagnosis has turned out to cause some of the very problems it was supposed to prevent—bone degeneration and fractures. A cynic might conclude that preventive medicine exists to transform people into raw material for a profit-hungry medical-industrial complex.

My first major defection from the required screening regimen was precipitated by a mammogram. No one likes mammography, which amounts to a brute-force effort to render the breasts transparent. First, a breast is flattened between two plates, then it is bombarded with ionizing radiation, which is, incidentally, the only environmental factor known for sure to cause breast cancer. I'd been fairly dutiful about mammograms since having been treated for breast cancer at the turn of the millennium, and now, about ten years later, the gynecologist's office reported that I'd had a "bad mammogram." I spent the next few anxious weeks undergoing further tests, in the midst of which I managed to earn a ticket for "distracted driving." Naturally I was distracted—by the looming decision of whether I would undergo debilitating cancer treatments again, or just let the disease take its course this time.

It turned out, after I'd been through a sonogram and fought panic in a coffinlike MRI tube, that the "bad mammogram" was a false positive resulting from the highly sensitive new digital forms of imaging. That was my last mammogram. Lest this seem like a reckless decision, I was supported in it by a high-end big-city oncologist, who viewed all my medical images and said that there would be no need to see me again, which I interpreted as ever again.

After this, every medical or dental encounter seemed to end in a tussle. Dentists—and I have met a number of them in my moves around the country—always wanted a fresh set of X-rays, even if the only problem was a chip in the tip of a tooth. All I could think of was the X-ray machines every shoe store had offered in my youth, through which children were encouraged to peer at the bones of their feet while wiggling their toes. The fun ended in the 1970s, when these "fluoroscopes" were eventually banned as dangerous sources of radiation. So why should I routinely expose my mouth, which is much more cancer-prone than the feet, to high annual doses of roentgens? If there was some reason to suspect underlying structural problems, okay, but just to satisfy the dentist's curiosity or meet some abstract "standard of care"—no.

In all these encounters, I was struck by the professionals' dismissal of my subjective reports—usually along the lines of "I feel fine"—in favor of the occult findings of their equipment. One physician, unprompted by any obvious signs or symptoms, decided to measure my lung capacity with the new handheld instrument he'd acquired for this purpose. I breathed into it, as instructed, as hard as I could, but my breath did not register on his screen. He fiddled with the instrument, looking deeply perturbed, and told me I seemed to be suffering from a pulmonary obstruction. In my defense, I argued that I do at least thirty minutes of aerobic exercise a day, not counting ordinary walking, but I was too polite to demonstrate that I was still capable of vigorous oral argument.

It was my dentist, oddly enough, who suggested, during an ordinary filling, that I be tested for sleep apnea. How a dentist got involved in what is normally the domain of ear, nose, and throat specialists, I do not know, but she recommended that the screening be done at a "sleep center," where I would attempt to sleep while heavily wired to monitoring devices, after which I could buy the treatment from her: a terrifying skull-shaped mask that would supposedly prevent sleep apnea and definitely extinguish any last possibility of sexual activity. But when I protested that there is no evidence I suffer from this disorder—no symptoms or detectable signs—the dentist said that I just might not be aware of it, adding that it could kill me in my sleep. This, I told her, is a prospect I can live with.

As soon as I reached the age of fifty physicians had begun to recommend—and in one case even plead—that I have a colonoscopy. As in the case of mammograms, the pressure to submit to a colonoscopy is hard to avoid. Celebrities promote them, comics snicker about them. During March, which is Colorectal Cancer Awareness Month, an eight-foot-high inflatable replica of a colon tours the country, allowing the anally curious to stroll through and inspect potentially cancerous polyps "from the inside."[2] But if mammography seems like a refined sort of sadism, colonoscopies mimic an actual sexual assault. First the patient is sedated—often with what is popularly known as the "date rape drug," Versed—then a long flexible tube, bearing a camera on one end, is inserted into the rectum and all the way up through the colon. What repelled me even more than this kinky procedure was the day of fasting and laxatives that was supposed to precede it, in order to ensure that the little camera encounters something other than feces. I put this off from year to year, until I finally felt safe in the knowledge that since colon cancer is usually slow-growing, any cancerous polyps I contain are unlikely to flourish until I am already close to death from other causes.

Then my internist, the chief physician in a midsized

group practice, sent out a letter announcing that he was suspending his ordinary practice in order to offer a new level of "concierge care" for those willing to cough up an extra $1,500 a year beyond what they already pay for insurance. The elite care would include twenty-four-hour access to the doctor, leisurely visits, and, the letter promised, all kinds of tests and screenings in addition to the routine ones. This is when my decision crystallized: I made an appointment and told him face-to-face that, one, I was dismayed by his willingness to drop his less-than-affluent patients, who appeared to make up much of the waiting room population. And, two, I didn't want more tests; I wanted a doctor who could *protect* me from unnecessary procedures. I would remain with the masses of ordinary, haphazardly screened patients.

Of course all this unnecessary screening and testing happens because doctors order it, but there is a growing rebellion within the medical profession. Overdiagnosis is beginning to be recognized as a public health problem, and is sometimes referred to as an "epidemic." It is an appropriate subject for international medical conferences and evidence-laden books like *Overdiagnosed: Making People Sick in the Pursuit of Health* by H. Gilbert Welch and his Dartmouth colleagues Lisa Schwartz and Steve Woloshin. Even health columnist Jane Brody, long a cheerleader for standard preventive care, now recommends that we think twice before undergoing what were once routine screening procedures. Physician and blogger John M. Mandrola advises straightforwardly:

Rather than being fearful of not detecting disease, both patients and doctors should fear healthcare. The best way to avoid medical errors is to avoid medical care. The default should be: I am well. The way to stay that way is to keep making good choices—not to have my doctor look for problems.[3]

With age, the cost/benefit analysis shifts. On the one hand, health care becomes more affordable—for Americans, anyway—at age sixty-five, when a person is eligible for Medicare. Exhortations to undergo screenings and tests continue, with loved ones joining the chorus. But in my case, the appetite for medical interactions of any kind wanes with each passing week. Suppose that preventive care uncovered some condition that would require agonizing treatments or sacrifices on my part—disfiguring surgery, radiation, drastic lifestyle limitations. Maybe these measures would add years to my life, but it would be a painful and depleted life that they prolonged. As it is now, preventive medicine often extends to the end of life: Seventy-five-year-olds are encouraged to undergo mammography; people already in the grip of one terminal disease may be subjected to screenings for others.[4] At a medical meeting, someone reported that a hundred-year-old woman had just had her first mammogram, causing the audience to break into a "loud cheer."[5]

One reason for the compulsive urge to test and screen and monitor is profit, and this is especially true in the United States, with its heavily private and often for-profit health system. How is a doctor—or hospital or drug company—to make money from essentially healthy patients? By subjecting them to tests and examinations that, in sufficient quantity, are bound to detect something wrong or at least worthy of follow-up. Gilbert and his coauthors offer a vivid analogy, borrowed from an expert in fractal geometry: "How many islands surround Britain's coasts?" The answer of course depends on the resolution of the map you are using, as well as how you are defining an "island." With high-resolution technologies like CT scans, the detection of tiny abnormalities is almost inevitable, leading to ever more tests, prescriptions, and doctor visits. And the tendency to overtest is amplified when the doctor who recommends the tests has a financial interest in the screening or imaging facility that he or she refers people to.

It's not only a profit-hungry medical system that drives overtesting and overdiagnosis. Individual consumers, that is, former and potential patients, may demand the testing and even threaten a malpractice suit if they feel it is being withheld. In the last couple of decades, "patient advocacy" groups have sprung up to "brand" dozens of diseases and publicize the need for screening. Many have their own celebrity spokespersons—Katie Couric for colorectal cancer, Rudy Giuliani for prostate cancer—and each sports its own distinctive colored ribbon—pink for breast cancer, purple for testicular cancer, black for melanoma, a "puzzle pattern" for autism, and so on—as well as special days or months for concentrated publicity and lobbying efforts. The goal of all this is generally "awareness," meaning a willingness to undergo the appropriate screening, such as mammograms and PSA tests.

There are even sizable constituencies for discredited tests. When the U.S. Preventive Services Task Force decided to withdraw its recommendation of routine mammograms for women under fifty, even some feminist women's health organizations, which I had expected to be more critical of conventional medical practices, spoke out in protest. A small band of women, identifying themselves as survivors of breast cancer, demonstrated on a highway outside the task force's office, as if demanding that their breasts be squeezed. In 2008, the same task force gave PSA testing a grade of "D," but advocates like Giuliani, who insisted that the test had saved his life, continued to press for it, as do most physicians.[6] Many physicians justify tests of dubious value by the "peace of mind" they supposedly confer—except of course on those who receive false positive results.

Thyroid cancer is particularly vulnerable to overdiagnosis. With the introduction of more high-powered imaging techniques, doctors were able to detect many more tiny lumps in people's necks and surgically remove them, whether surgery was warranted or not. An estimated 70 to 80 percent of thyroid cancer surgeries performed on US, French, and Italian women in the first decade of the twenty-first century are now judged to have been unnecessary. In South Korea, where doctors were especially conscientious about thyroid screening, the number rose to 90 percent. (Men were also overdiagnosed, but in far lower numbers.) Patients pay a price for these surgeries, including a lifelong dependence on thyroid hormones, and since these are not always fully effective, the patient may be left chronically "depressed and sluggish."[7]

So far I can detect no stirrings of popular revolt against the regime of unnecessary and often harmful medical screening. Hardly anyone admits to personally rejecting tests, and one who did—science writer John Horgan in a *Scientific American* blog on why he will not undergo a colonoscopy—somewhat undercut his well-reasoned argument by describing himself as an "anti-testing nut."[8] Most people joke about the distastefulness of the recommended procedures, while gamely submitting to whatever is expected of them.

But there's a significant rebellion brewing on another front. Increasingly, we read laments about the "medicalization of dying," usually focused on a formerly frisky parent or grandparent who had made clear her request for a natural, nonmedical death, only to end up tethered by cables and tubes to an ICU bed. Physicians see this all the time—witty people silenced by ventilators, the fastidious rendered incontinent—and some are determined not to let the same thing happen to themselves. They may refuse care, knowing that it is more likely to lead to disability than health, like the orthopedist who upon receiving a diagnosis of pancreatic cancer immediately closed down his practice and went home to die in relative comfort and peace.[9] A few physicians are more decisively proactive, and have themselves tattooed "NO CODE" or "DNR," meaning "do not resuscitate." They reject the same drastic end-of-life measures that they routinely inflict on their patients.

In giving up on preventive care, I'm just taking this line of thinking a step further: Not only do I reject the torment of a medicalized death, but I refuse to accept a medicalized life, and my determination only deepens with age. As the time that remains to me shrinks, each month and day becomes too precious to spend in windowless waiting rooms and under the cold scrutiny of machines. Being old enough to die is an achievement, not a defeat, and the freedom it brings is worth celebrating.

CHAPTER TWO

Rituals of Humiliation

Like most young women of my class and generation, I first became entangled with the medical profession when I reached my reproductive years, originally through the need for contraception. The major contraceptive available at the time was the diaphragm—a low-tech barrier method that required no great medical expertise to administer. But to win the medical profession's support for the legalization of birth control, Margaret Sanger had conceded the prescribing of diaphragms and other methods of birth control entirely to physicians. So at the age of about eighteen I was forced for the first time into the lithotomy position for, of course, a male gynecologist, to undergo a procedure I found extremely degrading. About a decade later, pregnancy ensnared me into regular monthly doctor visits, culminating a couple of weeks before the birth itself in a pelvic examination performed by the chief of obstetrics at the clinic I attended. No words were exchanged until, when the speculum had been removed from my vagina, I inquired whether my cervix was beginning to dilate. He looked at the nurse and asked in an arch tone, "Where did a nice girl like this learn to talk like that?"

Whether this exam had any effect on my—or, more important, my unborn child's—well-being, I have no idea, but its emotional impact was instantaneous. I was infuriated. Not only had I read the standard mass market books on pregnancy, but I had recently received a PhD in cell biology and could have gone on and on in what would have seemed to the obstetric chief a similarly obscene fashion. This, I should observe, is the moment I became a feminist in the fullest sense—a conscious woman, that is, and something other than an object or moron. The nurse, to her eternal credit, remained silent and poker-faced.

In the following years, I never questioned the need for regularly scheduled prenatal care, postnatal care, well-baby and then well-child care. I was a good mother and showed up as required for all the vaccinations and measurements of my children's growth. There were hints along the way, though, that something was going on other than the provision of necessary care. When a pediatrician prescribed my second child an antibiotic for a cold, I asked whether she had a reason to believe his illness was bacterial. "No, it's viral, but I always prescribe an antibiotic for a nervous mother." The prescribing was, in other words, a performance for my benefit. Muttering that I was not the one who was going to be taking it, I picked up my baby and left.

If a medical procedure has no demonstrable effect on a person's physiology, then how should that procedure be classified? Clearly it is a ritual, which can be defined very generally as a "solemn ceremony consisting of a series of actions performed according to a prescribed order."[1] But rituals can also have intangible psychological effects, so the question becomes whether those effects in some way contribute to well-being, or serve to deepen the patient's sense of helplessness or, in my case, rage.

Western anthropologists found indigenous people worldwide performing supposedly health-giving rituals that had no basis in Western science, often involving drumming, dancing, chanting, the application of herbal concoctions, and the manipulation of what appear to be sacred objects, such as animal teeth and colorful feathers. Anthropologist Edith Turner in the 1980s offered a lengthy and lovingly detailed account of the Ihamba ritual performed by the Ndembu of Zambia.[2] The afflicted person, whose symptoms include joint pains and extreme lassitude, is given a leaf infusion to drink, then her back is repeatedly anointed with other herbal mixtures, cut with a razor blade, and cupped with an animal horn—accompanied by drumming, singing, and a recital of grudges the patient holds against others in the village—until the source of the illness, the Ihamba, exits her body.

Does this ritual work? Yes, insofar as the afflicted person is usually restored to his or her usual strength and good humor. But there is no way to compare the efficacy of the Ihamba ritual to the measures a Western physician might use—the blood tests, the imaging, and so on—in part because the Ihamba itself is not something accessible to scientific medicine. It is conceived as the tooth of a human hunter, which has made its way into the victim's body, where it "bites" and may even reproduce. If this sounds fantastical, consider that, as an agent of disease, a "hunter's tooth" is a lot easier to visualize than a virus. Sometimes at the end of the ceremony one of the officiants will even produce a human tooth, claiming to have extracted it from the victim's body. And of course the opportunity to air long-held grudges may be therapeutic in itself.

Most of us would readily recognize the Ihamba ceremony as a "ritual"—a designation we would not be so quick to apply to a mammogram or a biopsy. The word carries a pejorative weight that is not associated with, for example, the phrase "health care." Early anthropologists could have called the healing practices of so-called primitive peoples "health care," but they took pains to distinguish the native activities from the purposeful interventions of Euro-American physicians. The latter were thought to be rational and scientific, while the former were "mere" rituals, and the taint of imperialist arrogance has clung to the word ever since. As a British medical anthropologist points out:

> The old anthropological approach to ritual relied upon a distinction between two kinds of action: that, on the one hand, which was ends-directed and reasonable from the anthropologist's point of view—and which might be described as related to skill, technique or craft—and, on the other, action which was apparently irrational and, as far as the anthropologist was concerned, did not reveal any such links. Only the second kind of action was to be thought of as ritual.[3]

Inevitably, a parallel was drawn between the healing rituals of supposedly primitive peoples and the procedures of modern Western medicine. The latter also take place in specially designated spaces and are usually performed by costumed personnel, wearing white coats and sometimes masks, who also manipulate objects generally unavailable to the public at large. In 1956, a time of widespread reverence for the medical profession and its institutional settings, an American anthropologist published an article cunningly entitled "Body Rituals Among the Nacirema"—"American" spelled backward. Describing the hospital as the "temple" where Nacireman healing rituals are performed, the essay recounts that

> few supplicants [patients] in the temple are well enough to do anything but lie on their hard beds. The daily ceremonies, like the rites of the holy-mouth-men [dentists], involve discomfort and torture. With ritual precision, the vestals awaken their miserable charges each dawn and roll them about on their beds of pain while performing ablutions, in the formal movements of which the maidens are highly trained. At other times they insert magic wands in the supplicant's mouth or force him to eat substances which are supposed to be healing. From time to time the medicine men come to their clients and jab magically treated needles into their flesh. The fact that these temple ceremonies may not cure, and may even kill the neophyte, in no way decreases the people's faith in the medicine men.[4]

The entire smorgasbord of procedures that make up the traditional "annual physical exam" can be seen as a ritual.

Introduced in the 1920s and recommended by the American Medical Association about a decade later, the annual physical loomed as a high-stress hurdle in the life of any health-conscious medical consumer, a trial, so to speak, to determine innocence (health) or guilt (disease). The ingredients of the annual physical are not well defined, and they can take from fifteen minutes to—in the case of the wealthy and hypochondriacal—several days. Yet health insurers required them as a condition of coverage, members of the military were subjected to them, ordinary healthy people were reminded by postcard to show up for them. What follows in the doctor's office resembles a religious ritual, or even a spectacle designed for entertainment. Commenting on the occasional deployment of clowns to cheer up pediatric hospital patients, one canny observer noted the parallels between these newcomers to the medical scene, "primitive" shamans, and the usual physicians, right down to the "unusual costumes," and even masks, worn by all of them.[5] The patient undresses, the "healer" (or clown or shaman) utters incantations and performs various actions on the patient's body. Then, in the medical case, comes the "confession," in which the patient is grilled as to his or her personal transgressions: Do they smoke? Drink? Take illegal drugs? Have multiple sex partners? I made the mistake once of admitting to some nonstandard drug use, years earlier, during college, but the feverish gleam that appeared in the doctor's eyes, along with a sudden burst of note-taking, convinced me never to mention it to a physician again.

The Emotional Impact of Ritual

To call something a "ritual" is not to say very much. Human rituals have ranged from human sacrifice to the innocent joys of maypole dancing, from forcible expulsion of a scapegoat from the community to the hearty embrace of a new leader or ally. But to say that a set of actions is a ritual does at least suggest that these actions serve social or cultural purposes other than the immediate task at hand, such as healing the sick or extracting an errant hunter's tooth. Twentieth-century anthropologists debated the "functions" of the rituals they found native people enacting—whether, for example, they served the individual participant or the group, the average person or, in hierarchical societies, the elite. Many rituals seemed designed to provide reassurance and guidance to individuals during various stages of the life cycle, such as puberty, which may be marked by painful scarification or by gentle celebrations like a bar mitzvah or a fifteen-year-old Latina girl's *quinceañera*. Other widespread rituals seemed designed to promote cohesion among individuals within a village or tribe—most obviously through group singing, dance, and feasting. Just as in traditional societies, modern urban people occupy a dense landscape of ritual—rituals of greeting and departure, holiday rituals, rituals associated with weddings, births, and deaths—most of which, most of the time, seem entirely benign. The psychological effect of these familiar rituals is usually to make the participants feel better about themselves and more securely bound to the community.

So what are the intangible effects of medical rituals? Do

they "empower," to use the popular verb, the objects of the rituals—that is, the patients—or contribute to a sense of helplessness and defeat?

One thing that stands out about medical procedures, as opposed to so many of the rituals we are likely to engage in, is that they tend to be transgressive, which is to say that they often violate accepted social norms. For example, we do not normally penetrate other people's "space" or allow others to do that to us, nor do we usually expose our undressed bodies to other people's inspection. Other, nonmedical rituals may be similarly transgressive, such as those involved in college fraternity and sports teams' hazings, where the initiate may be required to drink dangerous amounts of alcohol, take off his clothes, and undergo ritualized forms of sexual abuse. Then there are the peculiar rituals associated with the military, such as the drinking rituals of the British army, which include the formation of a "daisy chain" or "ring of soldiers connected through anal penetration." Participants justify this as a means of promoting group solidarity,[6] as could be said, I suppose, of far milder forms of collective rule-breaking as well.

Physicians have an excuse for flouting the normal rules of privacy: The human body is their domain, sometimes seen, in the case of women's bodies, as their exclusive property. In the middle of the twentieth century, no woman, at least no heterosexual laywoman, was likely to ever see her own or other women's genitalia, because that territory—aka "down there"—was reserved for the doctor. When in 1971 a few bold women introduced the practice of "cervical self-examination," performed with a plastic speculum, a flashlight, and a mirror, they were breaking two taboos—appropriating a medical tool (the speculum) and going where only doctors (or perhaps intimate partners) had gone before. Many doctors were outraged, with one arguing that in lay hands a speculum was unlikely to be sterile, to which feminist writer Ellen Frankfort replied cuttingly that yes, of course, anything that enters the vagina should first be boiled for at least ten minutes.[7]

Well before the revival of feminism in the 1970s, some American women had begun to complain about the heavy-handed overmedicalization of childbirth. In the middle of the century, it was routine for obstetricians to heavily sedate or even fully anesthetize women in labor. Babies were born to unconscious women, and the babies sometimes came out partially anesthetized themselves—sluggish and having difficulty breathing. Since the anesthetized or sedated woman could not adequately use her own muscles to push the baby out, forceps were likely to be deployed, sometimes leading to babies with cranial injuries. There was, however, an alternative, though obstetricians did not encourage it and often actively discouraged it: the Lamaze method, which had originated in the Soviet Union and France, offered breathing techniques that could reduce pain while keeping the mother and baby alert. In the 1960s, growing numbers of educated young women were taking Lamaze classes and demanding to remain awake during birth. By the time of my first pregnancy in 1970, it would have seemed irresponsible, at least in my circle of friends, to do anything else.

We were beginning to see that the medical profession, at the time still over 90 percent male, had transformed child-

birth from a natural event into a surgical operation performed on an unconscious patient in what approximated
a sterile environment. Routinely, the woman about to give
birth was subjected to an enema, had her pubic hair shaved
off, and was placed in the lithotomy position—on her back,
with knees up and crotch spread wide open. As the baby began to emerge, the obstetrician performed an episiotomy, a
surgical enlargement of the vaginal opening, which had to
be stitched back together after birth. Each of these procedures came with a medical rationale: The enema was to prevent contamination with feces; the pubic hair was shaved
because it might be unclean; the episiotomy was meant
to ease the baby's exit. But each of these was also painful,
both physically and otherwise, and some came with their
own risks. Shaving produces small cuts and abrasions that
are open to infection; episiotomy scars heal more slowly
than natural tears and can make it difficult for the woman
to walk or relieve herself for weeks afterward. The lithotomy position may be more congenial for the physician
than kneeling before a sitting woman, but it impedes the
baby's progress through the birth canal and can lead to tail-
bone injuries in the mother.

So how are we to think of these procedures, which some
doctors still insist on? If a procedure is not, strictly speaking, medically necessary to a healthy birth and may even
be contraindicated, why is it being performed? Anthropologist Robbie E. Davis-Floyd proposed that these interventions be designated as *rituals*, in the sense that they are no
more scientifically justified than the actions of a "primitive"
healer. They do not serve any physiological purpose, only

what she calls "ritual purposes." The enema and shaving underscore the notion that the woman is an unclean and even unwelcome presence in the childbirth process. Anesthesia and the lithotomy position send "the message that her body is a machine,"[8] or as Davis-Floyd quotes philosopher Carolyn Merchant, "a system of dead, inert particles," in which the conscious patient has no role to play. These are, in other words, rituals of domination, through which a woman at the very peak of her biological power and fecundity is made to feel powerless, demeaned, and dirty.

In one sense, childbirth rituals "worked." The women giving birth were often traumatized, reporting to Davis-Floyd that they "felt defeated"[9] or "thrown into depression": "You know, treating you like you're not very bright, like you don't know what's going on with your own body."[10] Yet, having submitted to so much discomfort and disrespect, they were expected to feel grateful to the doctor for a healthy baby. It was a perfect recipe for inducing women's compliance with their accepted social role: rituals of humiliation followed by the fabulous "gift" of a child.

But often, as in my own case, the rituals backfired and left women infuriated by their treatment during pregnancy and childbirth. It isn't easy to protest from the lithotomy position, but, in effect, growing numbers of women were rising to their feet and refusing the required medical interventions, even opting for homebirths and midwives. By the time my children hit two-digit ages, a nationwide women's health movement was challenging the misogyny it diagnosed in so much of women's care—from hazardous contraceptives to a barbarous form of breast cancer surgery, the Halsted radical mastectomy, that left its victims partially crippled. We managed to reform hospital obstetrical practice, winning acceptance for the Lamaze method, demanding and getting more female doctors, and asserting our right to participate in decisions throughout the process.

But just as we made these gains, obstetric care was becoming more intrusive and controlling in other ways. Electronic fetal monitoring during labor became routine even for low-risk births, and when the monitoring was conducted internally, through a probe inserted through the vagina, the woman had to remain bedridden throughout labor. Slight fluctuations in fetal heart rate could set off disproportionate alarm, leading to a shockingly high rate of caesarean sections—30 percent—that began to level off only in 2009. No longer could we place all the blame for the mismanagement of childbirth on "patriarchy." Women were also up against technocracy, as Davis-Floyd writes, and the idea that any procedure involving wires, drugs, and scalpels was inherently superior to anything that proceeded without technological intervention.

Even at the height of the Women's Health Movement, we hesitated to extend the feminist critique to those aspects of care that are not specific to women. True, on the academic and New Agey fringes of the movement, there were plenty of women who began to lump together patriarchy, technology, science, and imperialism into a single monolith bent on universal domination. Most of us, though, claimed science for our side, and took it as our mission to restore scientific rationality to a medical enterprise contaminated by sexism. We tended to assume that aside from women's care, medicine was relatively unbiased and neutral in its social impact.

Not so, argued social critic Ivan Illich in his 1975 book *Medical Nemesis*, which documented the negative effects of medical care on both sexes, in particular the toll of iatrogenic illnesses, that is, those induced by pharmaceuticals and the medical procedures themselves. Furthermore, he stated that medical institutions represent a vast system of social control, ruled by an "educated elite":

> Medicine has the authority to label one man's complaint a legitimate illness, to declare a second man sick though he himself does not complain, and to refuse a third social recognition of his pain, his disability.[11]

Like women, men who were not members of the educated elite—poor or working-class men—often faced a hostile and condescending medical profession. In a 1976 article, sociologist Irving K. Zola offered the case of his own father, a blue-collar worker who was advised by his physician to switch to a "desk job"—as if that were a possibility. Zola, an avid supporter of the Women's Health Movement, saw male as well as female patients being required to enact a ritual of deference to the doctor and the bureaucracy he was embedded in:

> Whether it be horizontal or in some awkward placement on one's back or stomach, legs splayed or cramped, or even in front of a desk, the patient is placed in a series of passive, dependent, and often humiliating positions.[12]

According to critical thinkers like Zola and Illich, one of the functions of medical ritual is social control. Medical encounters occur across what is often a profound gap in social status: Despite the last few decades' surge in immigrant and female doctors, the physician is likely to be an educated and affluent white male, and the interaction requires the patient to exhibit submissive behavior—to undress, for example, and be open to penetration of his or her bodily cavities. These are the same sorts of procedures that are normally undertaken by the criminal justice system, with its compulsive strip searches, and they are not intended to bolster the recipient's self-esteem. Whether consciously or not, the physician and patient are enacting a ritual of domination and submission, much like the kowtowing required in the presence of a Chinese emperor.

Some physicians, unsurprisingly, see medical rituals very differently. Instead of defending their procedures as scientific and invoking their personal experience as a form of "evidence" every bit as worthy as statistics, they defend ritual as the core of the medical encounter. Patients may care about a "cure," but they are even more intent on engaging in a ritual. One of the loudest proponents of medical ritual is Stanford medical professor Abraham Verghese, who wrote in a *New York Times* op-ed that most patients expect certain procedures when the doctor sees them, "and they are quick to perceive when he or she gives those procedures short shrift by, say, placing the stethoscope on top of the gown instead of the skin, doing a cursory prod of the belly and wrapping up in 30 seconds. Rituals are about transformation, the crossing of a threshold, and in the case of the bedside exam, the transformation is the cementing of the doctor-patient relationship."[13]

And what is the nature of this relationship? As he expands in a TED talk, it is a relationship based on the patient's submission to inquiries and physical contact that would normally be seen as rude or, worse, assaultive:

> Well I would submit to you that the ritual of one individual coming to another and telling them things that they would not tell their preacher or rabbi, and then, incredibly on top of that, disrobing and allowing touch—I would submit to you that that is a ritual of exceeding importance.[14]

This is, to say the least, a muddled proposition: Is the ritual necessary to soften whatever discomfort might be caused by the intimacies required for good medical care? Or is it the other way around—that the intimacies are required to heighten the drama of the ritual? Apparently the intimacies may in no way be required for successful care, but patients—always unnamed, of course—demand them anyway. Verghese offers an anecdote about a breast cancer patient who had gone for her treatment to what she judged to be "the best cancer center in the world," only to return a few months later to the less prestigious facility where she had been diagnosed. He runs into her there and asks, "Why did you come back and get your care here?"

> And she was reluctant to tell me. She said, "The cancer center was wonderful. It had a beautiful facility, giant atrium, valet parking, a piano that played itself, a concierge that

took you around from here to there. But," she said, "but they did not touch my breasts." Now you and I could argue that they probably did not need to touch her breasts. They had her scanned inside out. They understood her breast cancer at the molecular level; they had no need to touch her breasts.[15]

Here the defense of medical ritual verges creepily on the excuse commonly offered by sexual assailants: "She was asking for it."

None of which is to say that human interactions—including rituals and touch—play no role in health care. Think of the mother's kiss that magically relieves a toddler's boo-boo or the reassurance that emanates from a concerned and kindly health care provider. Our bodies are not cadavers; they are inhabited by our minds, through which we are connected to other humans and animals both living and dead. Strengthen those connections and we are likely to feel better. Threaten or sever them and the result could be fatal, as in cases of "voodoo death," widely observed in traditional societies, where a person who has received a death curse or broken a powerful taboo dies within a day or so for no apparent physical reason.

There is hard evidence for the efficacy of ritual displays of concern in the form of the well-documented placebo effect: Patients given a sham treatment—say, a sugar pill—are more likely to feel better than those given no treatment, real or fake, at all. In one study, those who received a fake treatment along with care described by the experimenter as "very schmaltzy," with elaborate expressions of concern

("I'm so glad to meet you"; "I know how difficult this is for you") while being touched on their hands and shoulders, did better than those who had been given their placebo in a more brusque and impersonal fashion.[16] This result was attributed by some to "positive thinking"—if you expect that an intervention will help, it probably will.

But then the experimenter, Ted Kaptchuk of Harvard Medical Services, eliminated the effect of positive expectations: He and his team told a subgroup of patients that what they were being given was in fact a placebo, "like a sugar pill." "Not only did we make it absolutely clear that these pills had no active ingredient and were made from inert substances, but we actually had 'placebo' printed on the bottle." To the researchers' surprise, the patients who knowingly took the placebo experienced improvements comparable to those who took a real, FDA-approved medicine for their condition (irritable bowel syndrome). "These findings," says Kaptchuk, suggest "that there may be significant benefit to the very performance of medical ritual."[17]

Physicians who, like Verghese, emphasize the importance of the medical encounter as a ritualized interaction may take comfort from these placebo studies. From a scientific standpoint, though, they cast yet another awkward light on the epistemology of medicine. The idea, going back at least to the turn of the twentieth century, had been that medical procedures were entirely rational, with each step dictated by well-tested biomedical principles. Everyone acknowledged a role for incalculable factors like "schmaltz" or "bedside manner," but this role was thought to be auxiliary to the main event—the surgery, administration of pharmaceuticals, or interventions of scientifically proven value. But if what the patient really needs, at least in some cases, is attention and some display of concern, why is the practice of medicine limited to laboratory-trained physicians operating in massively capital-intensive medical institutions?

Well, it could be argued that science, or the veneer of science, is required to make a ritual acceptable to modern, educated people, who are unlikely to be impressed by drumming and animal horns. The Ihamba ritual may be the culturally appropriate way for the Ndembu people to express concern for an afflicted person; Westerners require the trappings of big science—imaging machines, centrifuges, and sterile, or at least blank, interior rooms. But to my knowledge no one has tested this proposition. Would it help to add cut flowers, soothing music, and friendlier faces to the conventional medical encounter? Does all the equipment have to be real, or would cardboard imitations do just as well? And if the real point of medical ritual is to demonstrate social support for the patient, surely we could do so in ways that are less grotesquely expensive, as well as less stressful and demeaning.

CHAPTER THREE

The Veneer of Science

What gives medicine its authority is the presumption that it is based on science. A few centuries ago, the major source of intellectual and moral authority in Western culture was religion, which requires that you put your trust in some distant personage like Jesus or Mohammed because large numbers of other people who are thought to be trustworthy already do so. Science was a big improvement in that it does not require trust, which rests on social conformity, but offers a way of verifying things for yourself. I know that any scientific claim I encounter—whether about the moons of Jupiter or the best way to treat a fever—can in principle be tested by repeating the observations made by scientists. No belief is required, only patience and the infinite humility it takes to learn daunting forms of mathematics and biology. If the claim cannot be verified by independent observers, if it is, in other words, "irreproducible," we are forced to conclude that it is not true.

Since most of us are unlikely to learn enough math to calculate the orbits of Jupiter's moons, we tend to defer to those who have, at least in planetary lunar matters. Similarly, modern, educated people are usually intimidated by the mere invocation of science. We want remedies that are "scientifically proven" and can bear up under the phrase "studies show." So in the medical case, if a person previously unknown to you requested that you undress and submit to his or her probings, you would be unlikely to comply. But if that person could justify their request with decades of experience and peer-reviewed studies showing that this procedure had contributed to the longevity and well-being of large numbers of others—well, then, it might be wise to do what is asked of you. The medical profession won its monopoly over the business of healing by invoking its scientific basis, and maintained that monopoly by diligently patrolling its borders against the alternatives, long described as "pseudoscience." A little more than a century ago, the matter appeared to be settled when nonphysicians were legally barred from practicing, which in the United States meant outlawing midwifery in favor of obstetrics and marginalizing homeopathy in favor of "allopathic," aka "regular" or scientific, medicine.

Only slowly did any kind of real détente arise, with the AMA-style doctors gradually softening their invective against alternatives. As late as the 1950s, the American Cancer Society, which is about as medically conventional as a health-related group could be, still had a "Committee on Quackery." But according to *Harvard* magazine:

Later that [committee] turned into a committee on "unproven methods of cancer management," superseded by one on "questionable methods." The names indicate a gradual acceptance of the unconventional; today the cancer society has a Committee on Complementary and Alternative Medicine (CAM). The evolving vocabulary also reflects a sea change underway throughout medicine. In the last few years, the term "alternative," suggesting something done *instead of* conventional medicine, has been giving way to "complementary," a therapy done *along with* mainstream treatment. Both words may ultimately be replaced by "integrative medicine"—the use of techniques like acupuncture, massage, herbal treatments, and meditation in regular medical practice.[1]

This may look like commendable humility on the part of conventional medicine—or it may look like a shameless compromise. But how scientific is conventional "scientific" medicine anyway? By the late twentieth century, mathematically oriented physicians, as well as many patients, were beginning to ask for something more than a doctor's word for the efficacy of medical interventions and something more tangible than the mere aura of science. They wanted hard evidence, and one familiar procedure after another has come up short.

In 1974, a former physician turned mathematician, David M. Eddy, was asked to give a talk on medical decision making, and chose to focus on diagnostic mammography since Betty Ford's and Happy Rockefeller's breast cancers were very much in the news at the time. Years later, he wrote that he had "planned to write out the decision tree I presumed their physicians had used, fully expecting to find strong evidence, good numbers, and sound reasoning that

I could describe to my audience. But to my amazement I found very few numbers, no formal rationale, and blatant errors in reasoning. How could that be?"[2]

He decided to try to study the decision making behind something that had been around much longer than mammography—a seventy-five-year-old treatment for ocular hypertension that had been used on tens of millions of people. But he could find only eight controlled studies—meaning studies comparing people who had received the treatment to a group of similar people who had not—and these studies were all "very small and poorly designed." Worse, six of them found that the recipients of treatment ended up worse off than those who had not received it. Eddy moved on to analyze other treatments, only to be warned off by experts who told him there was not enough data to work on.

> That clinched it. If there wasn't sufficient information to develop a decision tree, what in the world were physicians basing their decisions on? I then realized that medical decision making was not built on a bedrock of evidence or formal analysis, but was standing on Jell-O.[3]

So began what was soon called "evidence-based medicine," the idea that anything performed on patients should be backed up by statistical evidence. This was a provocative designation, raising the immediate question of what medicine had been based on up until now: anecdotes, habits, hunches? Or was medicine traditionally not "evidence-based" but "eminence-based," that is, backed by the reputations and institutional standing of the people who practiced it?

Most of the medical screenings that have been pressed on me by one health professional or another fail the evidence-based test. Mammograms, for example: The conventional wisdom, tirelessly repeated by the leading breast cancer advocacy group, the Susan G. Komen Foundation, was that early detection through annual mammography would significantly increase the five-year survival rate from breast cancer.[4] But repeated, huge, often international studies showed no significant decline in breast cancer mortality that could be attributed to routine mammographic screening. True, any woman whose cancer had been detected through screening might claim to have been saved by the intervention, but the likelihood was that the spot in her mammogram would never have developed into full-blown cancer. What screening was finding, and doctors were treating, were often slow-growing or inactive tumor sites—or even noninvasive conditions like the wrongly named "ductal cancer in situ," or DCIS. Treating pre-cancers and non-cancers may seem like a commendable excess of caution, except that the treatments themselves— surgery, chemotherapy, and radiation—entail their own considerable risks. Disturbingly enough, breast biopsies are themselves a risk factor for cancer and can "seed" adjacent tissue with cancer cells.[5]

The same kinds of concerns apply to screening for prostate cancer, which consists of a blood test for prostate-specific antigen (PSA) plus a digital rectal exam. As with mammography, statistical studies have found no overall decrease in mortality that can be attributed to the PSA screening that has been in place since the late 1980s.[6] Here too, the price can be high for overdiagnosis and treatment: radiation and hormonal therapies that can lead to incontinence, impotence, and cardiovascular disease.[7] In 2011, the U.S. Preventive Services Task Force recommended that men no longer receive PSA tests, and two years later the American Urological Association grudgingly followed suit, limiting PSA screening to men between the ages of fifty-five and sixty-nine.[8] As for colonoscopies, they may detect potentially cancerous polyps, but they are excessively costly in the United States—up to $10,000—and have been found to be no more accurate than much cheaper, noninvasive tests such as examination of the feces for traces of blood.[9]

There is an inherent problem with cancer screening: It has been based on the assumption that a tumor is like a living creature, growing from small to large and, at the same time, from innocent to malignant. Hence the emphasis on "staging" tumors, from zero to four, based on their size and whether there is evidence of any metastasis throughout the body. As it turns out, though, size is not a reliable indicator of the threat level. A small tumor may be highly aggressive, just as a large one may be "indolent," meaning that a lot of people are being treated for tumors that will likely never pose any problem. One recent study found that almost half the men over sixty-six being treated for prostate cancer are unlikely to live long enough to die from the disease anyway.[10] They will, however, live long enough to suffer from the adverse consequences of their treatment.

The physical part of the annual physical is largely determined by the individual physician and of course the insurance company or other institution underwriting the exam. According to the Canadian Task Force on Preventive Health Care, "It consisted of a head-to-toe physical examination and the use of whatever tests were available: blood count, urine glucose and protein, chest X-ray, and, since the 1950s, ECG, CT scans, and MRIs"[11]—and I would add an emphasis on "whatever." In the 1940s and '50s, when there were more US hospital beds than could be filled by the injured or ill, affluent patients could expect to be hospitalized for their annual exams, the better to anesthetize them for invasive procedures. At the other end of the class spectrum, more or less, pre-induction medical exams for the military were notably sketchy, usually consisting of a hearing and vision test, plus a quick inspection for hemorrhoids and open lesions. In between these extremes, most people had their vital signs taken, their urine and blood worked up, their breasts or testicles palpated, perhaps with a digital rectal exam thrown in. In 2015, the cost of annual physicals was estimated at $10 billion a year.[12]

Women are supposed to undergo a second, gynecological annual exam, and this one has been well defined since its inception in the 1950s: breast and external genitalia exams, a Pap smear to detect cervical cancer, a vaginal and perhaps rectal exam. These exams are not always voluntarily undertaken; they may be required as a condition of obtaining or renewing a prescription for a contraceptive: Recall the searing scene in *Mad Men* where Peggy undergoes a gyn exam in order to get birth control pills and the (male) doctor cautions her that just because the pills are expensive, she shouldn't become "the town pump just to get [her] money's worth."[13] Many women are traumatized by these exams, which in their detailed attention to breasts and genitalia so closely mimic actual sexual encounters. Out-of-place intimacies, like unwelcome touching by a male coworker, are normally regarded as "sexual harassment," but the entire gyn exam consists of intimate touching, however disguised as a professional, scientifically justified procedure. And sometimes this can be a pretty thin disguise. A physician attached to an American missionary compound in Bangladesh is alleged to have molested girls, one as young as twelve, by subjecting them to almost daily breast and pelvic exams—procedures that are not normally performed on preteen girls.[14]

Even under the best, most "professional" circumstances, such exams can be deeply upsetting. According to one woman, writing on a site called *For Women's Eyes Only*, pelvic exams are "humiliating, degrading, and painful":

> The first time I had a pap smear done, I was so traumatized, I now have to take prescription Xanax to avoid having panic attacks when I get pap smears done now. And I'm only 24. How many more am I going to have to have for the rest of my life? What am I going to do when I want to have children and every doctor wants to shove his/her fingers and tools inside me?[15]

Other women strive for a state of psychological dissociation, attempting to share the physician's view of their body as a passive and unfeeling object, detached from a conscious mind.

One problem, though certainly not the only problem, with these regularly scheduled invasions of privacy is that they do not save lives or reduce the risk of illness. In 2014, the American College of Physicians announced that standard gyn exams were of no value for asymptomatic adult women and were certainly not worth the "discomfort, anxiety, pain and additional medical costs" they entailed.[16] As for the annual physical exams offered to both sexes, their evidentiary foundations had begun to crumble over forty years ago, to the point where a physician in 2015 could write that they were "basically worthless." Both types of exams can lead to false positives, followed by unnecessary tests and even surgery, or to a false sense of reassurance, since a condition that was undetectable at the time of the exam could blossom into a potentially fatal cancer within a few months. But such considerations do not seem to have deterred many physicians, like this one, quoted in a *New York Times* article entitled "Annual Physical Checkup May Be an Empty Ritual":

Dr. Barron Lerner, an internist and historian of medicine at Columbia University's College of Physicians and Surgeons, says he asks patients to come in every year and always listens to their heart and lungs, does a rectal exam, checks lymph nodes, palpates their abdomens and examines the breasts of his female patients.

"It's what I was taught and it's what patients have been taught to expect," he said, although he acknowledged he would be hard pressed to give a scientific justification for those procedures.[17]

None of the above should be construed as an attack on the notion of scientific medicine. True, the medical profession has again and again misused the authority conferred on it by science to justify unnecessary procedures for the sake of profits or simply to gratify physicians' egos (and, in the worst case, sexual impulses). But medicine's alliance with science has also brought incalculable benefits, from sterile technique in the operating room to lifesaving pharmaceuticals. The only cure for bad science is more science, which has to include both statistical analysis and some recognition that the patient is not "just a statistic," but a conscious, intelligent agent, just as the doctor is.

There remains a considerable market for "comprehensive" exams filled with tests and procedures that are no longer recommended, just as there is a luxury market for antique cars and vinyl records. I first encountered this phenomenon in the 1990s, when a wealthy acquaintance, unprompted by any symptoms, took off for a two-day-long medical exam at Johns Hopkins. Other, perhaps even wealthier, people opt for multiday exams combined with "spa services" and "lifestyle coaching" in luxury vacation settings. As of 2008, 22 percent of Fortune 500 companies provided "executive exams" to their top personnel,[18] both as a perk and as a way to avoid having a trusted leader die of a heart attack at his or her desk. But an article in the *Harvard Business Review* entitled "Executive Physicals: What's the ROI [Return on Investment]?" answers its own question with what amounts to a firm "not much"—and for all the reasons I have given here: the frequency of false positives, the dangers of the tests themselves (such as radiation), and the unlikelihood of finding a problem in a still-treatable stage.[19]

Mounting insistence on evidence-based medicine—some of it coming from the health insurance industry—led, in the early twenty-first century, to the perception that medicine was going through an "epistemological crisis," that is, a crisis in its intellectual foundations. In 2006 the noted bioethicist Arthur L. Caplan wrote:

> Contemporary medicine is sailing on very rocky seas these days. It is being buffeted by ever-rising costs, doubts about its efficacy, and intrusions on its turf from competitors that range from optometrists, psychologists, chiropractors, midwives, and nurse-anesthetists to the friendly folks at the herb and vitamin store.[20]

But, he went on, it was the "fervency of the embrace of evidence-based medicine"[21] that struck at the profession's core conceit: the notion that it was derived, at least since the late nineteenth century, from the arduous methods and processes of the hard sciences.

Laboratories and Cadavers

In fact, the relationship between medicine and science has always been tenuous. A hundred and fifty years ago, there was no American medical profession, only a collection of diverse men and women claiming healing skills, some with years of experience, but many with little more than an apprenticeship to go on. Only toward the end of the nineteenth century did it became fashionable for relatively elite college-educated doctors to round off their educations in Germany. There, they were entranced by the universities' gleaming new medical research labs, with their microscopes, test tubes, and well-scrubbed countertops, which had no analog in the United States. Laboratories are forbidding places to the uninitiated, showing few signs of human occupation except for the occasional stool and making no concessions to decoration. But to a scientist they represent a place where he (and at one time it was almost always "he") potentially exercised total control, with no disruptive breezes or temperature changes and hopefully no contaminants. It was the white coat of the laboratory scientist, the chemist, or the bacteriologist that physicians eventually adopted as a uniform suitable for encounters with patients. What it symbolizes is not only cleanliness, but mastery and control.

In a laboratory, the causes of disease could be traced to the cellular level and studied like any other natural phenomenon, hence the proclamation of the famed German researcher Rudolf Virchow that "medical practice is nothing but a minor offshoot of pathological physiology as developed in laboratories of animal experimentation."[22] This is of course an arguable proposition, but it immediately provided legitimation for a wave of professional reform in the United States: Medicine was the business of scientists, or at least of the scientifically trained, and no one should be legally certified to practice it without at least two years (now four) of college education and a thorough background in the laboratory sciences.

But the relevance of the scientific reforms in medical education to the actual practice of medicine remains unclear. For example, no one attains the right to practice medicine without studying organic chemistry in college—a course that pre-med students call the "weed-out course" since it eliminates so many aspirants to the medical profession. But organic chemistry, delightful as it may be from my point of view, has no obvious contribution to make to medicine. A comprehension of electron orbitals is not required for an understanding of the germ theory of disease, nor do you need to appreciate the structure of DNA to study genetic disorders. An obstetrician complained:

> The Krebs cycle is a classic example—a biochemical cycle where you have to learn all these enzymes and when you get through you never use it. My sister in med school now tells me the same thing. She can't understand why she is going through all these detailed analyses of DNA structures and things like that.[23]

But one likely effect of the scientific reform of medicine was to scare away any critical social scientists. Except for tongue-in-cheek offerings like "Body Rituals Among the Nacirema," none of the anthropologists and sociologists who took up the study of medical care in the mid- to late twentieth century dared to question the relative efficacy of "primitive" rituals and those of modern scientific medicine. They seem to have assumed that medical procedures, being based on scientific observations and methods, must be of proven value, even when those procedures looked suspiciously like "rituals." After all, the social sciences also considered themselves to be "sciences," and were habitually deferential to the medical profession, with its formidable armor of biochemistry and microbiology. No mere social scientist was prepared to weigh in on the question of whether particular medical procedures actually did any good.

Predictably enough, the medical reforms of the early twentieth century narrowed the demographic base of the medical profession. The requirement that medical schools possess laboratories eliminated most schools that had admitted women and African-Americans. Furthermore, at a time when only 5 percent of the population had a college degree, the requirement of at least some college limited medical school admissions to the upper and upper middle classes. No longer could any "crude boy or...jaded clerk," as one of the leading reformers described the run-of-the-mill doctors of his time,[24] expect to gain medical training. Doctors would be recruited from the class of "gentlemen," which was why even female patients could now entrust them with intimate access to their bodies. For most people, throughout most of the twentieth century, medical care necessarily involved an encounter with a social superior—a white male from a relatively privileged background.

With medicine anchored, at least symbolically, in laboratory science, the practice of medicine changed too. Medicine began to look like an "extractive industry," as health policy expert Robb Burlage once put it,[25] with the doctor's office serving as a collection site where blood, urine, and bits of tissue were converted into laboratory samples and hence into data. Or it might be images, like X-rays or CT scans, that are harvested, sometimes sent out for analysis, possibly to a distant country where radiologists are paid less. As the focus shifted to tissues and cells, physicians began to seem impatient with the intact human body. They wanted—and according to their training, needed—to reach inside, past the skin, to whatever pathologies lay within. Melvin Konner, an anthropologist turned medical student, described his first experience with surgery:

> My fingers had been inside another person's body, not just in the mouth or vagina or rectum, but beneath the protective surface of the skin, the inviolable film set up by millions of years of evolution, the envelope of ultimate individuality.... For me it had been an unforgettable experience.[26]

In the laboratory-centered environment, the patient's words—his or her medical history and reported symptoms—count for less than the objective data that instruments can collect. Recall my difficulty in convincing an internist that I could breathe perfectly well, despite the evidence from his brand-new device. At another time in my life, I had the opposite problem—trying to convince a doctor that my cardiac symptoms were "real," not psychosomatic (the problem was eventually diagnosed as non-life-threatening and treatable with a beta blocker). When you visit a doctor for the first time, you may be asked to show up half an hour early to give you time to fill out a lengthy history, but many of the questions will be asked again anyway, suggesting that your efforts went unread. Or they may be ignored. Thomas Duncan, the first person to die of Ebola in the United States, told an emergency room nurse that he had just arrived from Liberia, one of the epicenters of the epidemic, but that information never reached the attending physician, who sent Duncan home with instructions to take Tylenol.

It could be argued that the ideal patient says nothing, lies perfectly still, and makes no objection to the most invasive procedures. In fact, the first "patient" a medical student usually encounters is dead—a cadaver donated for dissection—and death is a condition that, as philosopher Jeffrey P. Bishop points out, is almost a prerequisite for scientific study: "After all, life is in flux, and it is difficult to make truth claims about matter in motion, about bodies in flux."[27] The heart is beating, blood is flowing, cells are metabolizing and even rushing about the living tissue. "Thus, life is no foundation upon which to build a true science of medicine," he continues.[28] This may sound like calculated irony, but consider how a "true science," like biology, actually works. Until very recent advances in microscopy, the study of life at the microscopic level required that you first kill a laboratory animal, remove the tissue you want to study, slice a bit of it very thin, then "fix" it by rendering it thoroughly dead—in fact embalmed—with formaldehyde. Only then is it ready to go on the glass slide that you will see through the microscope, although what you see will be only a distant approximation of living tissue within a living animal, just as a field strewn with dead bodies will give you little idea of the issues that led to war. Similarly, Bishop proposes that the dead body is "epistemologically normative" in medicine, since what goes on in living bodies is too blurry, ever-changing, and confusing for study.

Many physicians and social scientists have questioned the pedagogical value of cadaver dissection. After all, the cadaver is dead and artificially preserved; it is smelly, leathery, and utterly lacking in the "flux" that constitutes life. Some prestigious medical schools have abandoned it altogether, instead teaching anatomy on plastic "prosections" of body parts. But for the most part, American medical schools (though not Italian ones) still insist on cadaver dissection, going so far as to defend it as a "rite of passage," in which even the trauma that some medical students experience can be justified as a vital part of their transformation from initiate into full-fledged physician. Medical schools often attempt to "humanize" the process with little rituals of gratitude to the cadavers' donors, but dissection remains a violent and transgressive undertaking. As one bioethicist observes:

> One of the functions of anatomy lab is to help teach physicians how to violate social norms that operate in every other social situation, a skill that will be necessary in clinical practice. The detachment that allows student physicians to cut up the dead may help practicing clinicians to put their hands and medical instruments in patients' various bodily orifices or to ask patients to confess their most shameful secrets and expose their nakedness in the most vulnerable positions.[29]

Every profession requires a certain degree of detachment on the part of its practitioners, but in the case of medicine this affect may mask something darker. Konner, the anthropologist who became a medical student, observes that "the stress of clinical training alienates the doctor from the patient, that in a real sense the patient becomes the enemy."[30] The doctors-in-training, invariably exhausted, blow off steam by talking trash about their patients, who are of course the immediate cause of their woes—patients "blow" their IVs, as Konner mentions, or spike sudden fevers. Then too, the rushed pace of modern clinical practice, in which outpatients may be scheduled ten or fifteen minutes apart, contributes to the kind of resentment a retail worker feels in the face of a customer overload. The doctor's detachment is not a defense against excessive empathy, but a "downright negative" emotional stance, Konner suggests:

> To cut and puncture a person, to take his or her life in your hands, to pound the chest until the ribs break…these and a thousand other things may require something stronger than objectivity. They may actually require a measure of dislike.[31]

So it is ironic that it is the patient—the thinking, feeling, conscious patient, so long discounted or ignored—whom the medical profession has turned to as an ally against the threat of evidence-based medicine. When the epidemiologist points out the uselessness of a certain procedure, the physician counters that this is what his or her patients want and even demand. An internist in Burlington, North Carolina, reports that when he told a seventy-two-year-old patient that she did not need many of the tests she was expecting in her annual physical, she wrote a letter to the local paper complaining about him as an example of "socialized medicine."[32] What patients want, according to the foes of evidence-based medicine, is above all a highly stylized but human interaction with a doctor. As one physician argues:

> Medicine's theatrical trappings—the operating theaters, the costumes such as the doctor's white coat and the patient's Johnny gown, the formalized lines and gestures— all contribute to an aesthetic ritual which gives emotional meaning to doctor-patient contact that transcends the notion of a cure.[33]

There are arguments that can be made against an over-reliance on statistical evidence—that, for example, it may obscure a patient's unique constellation of problems. As the popular doctor-writer Jerome Groopman puts it, "Statistics cannot substitute for the human being before you; statistics embody averages, not individuals."[34] Another argument often deployed against evidence-based medicine is that it can become a tool of the insurance industry to limit the care that will be reimbursed. We should always err on the side of excessive care, medical liberals insist, rather than promoting a potentially dangerous austerity. So there are reasonable arguments against the uncritical adoption of evidence-based medicine. But the notion that it undermines an interaction that "transcends the notion of a cure" is not one of them.

CHAPTER FOUR

Crushing the Body

I f I seem to be rather cavalier about preventive medical care, it is in part because there are so many alternative pathways to health on offer in our thriving consumer culture. The very word "alternative" has acquired a certain zing, as in "alternative lifestyles," and especially "alternative medicine." Consider the disorienting multitude of options, all seemingly compatible and equally respectable, facing anyone seeking help for even the most routine problem, like lower back pain, which almost everyone suffers from at some point in their lives. A conventionally minded person might start with a referral to an orthopedist, who will usually make an effort to localize the problem in particular vertebrae that can, at least in some cases, be corrected surgically. Or, advised by a friend or magazine article, the patient might begin with an "alternative" healer such as a massage therapist or acupuncturist. Often these choices are available in the same setting, perhaps a major university hospital like that at the University of Maryland's Center for Integrative Medicine, where the menu includes reflexology, reiki, yoga, acupuncture, and "micronutrient infusions," as well as "physician care." Stanford's Center for Integrative Medicine, which offers, among other things, classes in mindfulness and "Positive Psychology: The Pursuit of Happiness," provides each patient with a three-member team representing both conventional and alternative medicine to guide them through the many possible treatment options. There are, however, no warning signs to alert the patient that these options have long represented warring sides—on the one side science, and on the other, any number of ancient, often religious traditions. Nor is there any clue that one's choice of treatment modalities is anything more than a matter of personal taste.

I had my own alternative—not "alternative medicine," but an alternative *to* medicine. I had begun to work out, to systematically use my body in what could be described as fairly useless ways that had nothing to do with house-cleaning or getting myself from one place to another. Early in the 1980s, a friend got me going with her to an unchallenging women's-only gym in a nearby shopping center. She wanted to lose weight; my lower backaches had forced me to realize I could no longer treat my body as mere scaffolding for keeping my head upright. It needed some work.

And I needed some play. Except for brief bursts of house-work, adult life, it turned out in my case, was conducted in the sitting position—in meetings or at a desk. The gym offered an enticing regressiveness, a chance, I wrote at the time, to reclaim "the lost muscular license of youth." We waved our arms, crunched our abs, or lay on the floor and raised our legs to the beat of Billy Idol's version of "Mony

Mony." After a day spent manipulating words and trying to coax paragraphs into an orderly sequence, forty-five minutes of zoned-out, militaristic obedience to the fitness instructor in front of the class seemed almost like freedom.

At first I was mortified by the feebleness of my body. But if I wasn't strong, I was at least possessed of a high tolerance for pain, so the mortification began to develop into a secret competitiveness. In normal life I like to think I am a modest and cooperative person; in the gym I was always covertly comparing myself to others and seething with ambition to outdo them. Soon I graduated from the women's-only gym to a large, lavishly equipped gym for both sexes, where I began with group classes—staying in the back of the room where I could observe without being observed—and then worked my way up to the weight room where the men worked out. All of this was completely removed from my normal professional and personal life and not even worth mentioning to anyone, I thought—too trivial and narcissistic. The first affirmation I got for all this effort was from a male friend who warned me that my upper arms were getting "scary."

There is no single satisfying historical explanation for the surge of interest in physical fitness that hit the United States in the late twentieth century and spread from there to other affluent parts of the world. One factor was simply the growing availability of fitness-inducing experiences, such as those offered by gyms. In the 1970s, the few gyms that existed tended to be no-frills weight rooms, not all of them even with showers. Today there are 186,000 health clubs worldwide, generating about $81 billion a year, of which about

$26 billion is spent in the United States, with Germany and Brazil not far behind.[1] Sometime in the 1980s, entrepreneurs discovered that after the initial investment in equipment, it did not take much effort to maintain a gym, only sufficient staff to keep the towels laundered and check clients' membership status when they enter the facility.

But the demand, as well as the supply, was increasing. In some ways, it was part of a larger withdrawal into individual concerns after the briefly thrilling communal uplift some had experienced in the 1960s. Self-help books proliferated to the point where they became a separate literary genre, as if a fashionable segment of the society had taken up a new project—themselves. Pop psych self-help books advised one to treat relationships as market transactions, always asking whether you're getting as much as you're giving. And if that wasn't working, you could always "be your own best friend." To historian Christopher Lasch, the fitness obsession was just another aspect of the "culture of narcissism," representing "a retreat from politics and a repudiation of the recent past."[2]

Lasch offered Jerry Rubin as an irrefutable exemplar of this retreat. Rubin had a sterling résumé as a radical activist—a flamboyant antiwar leader, a defendant in the "Chicago Seven" trial for inciting the "riots" at the 1968 Democratic convention, a founder, with Abbie Hoffman, of the anarchist Yippie movement. In 1969, he was telling college students that America's only choices were "catastrophe and decadence or revolution and a new life style,"[3] but in his case it was the new lifestyle that won out over the revolution. As the 1970s went on, he sampled every available New Age fad—EST, Rolfing, yoga, meditation—finally emerging as a proud capitalist entrepreneur and promoter of physical fitness. He saw himself not as a sellout, but as a role model for personal "growth." But there is a case to be made for Lasch's theory that the new self-involvement represented by fitness was in fact a kind of defeat. When the movement petered out, Rubin's erstwhile comrade Abbie Hoffman did not transform himself into a self-improvement guru or businessman. He committed suicide.

Of course most of the young, educated people who started jogging and gym-going in the 1970s and '80s had never expected, much less worked to bring about, a political and cultural revolution. But they had hoped for stable employment, preferably in jobs they found meaningful and creative, and in an age when the entire sociological map was being redrawn, there was little chance of that. First, the traditional blue-collar working class gave way to "deindustrialization," meaning plant closings and layoffs. As the downsizing fervor spread to the nonprofit sector, whole sections of the professional middle class crumbled off like calves from a melting iceberg. Human service agencies began to shed their social workers, psychologists, and public-interest lawyers. Universities shuttered departments, like philosophy and foreign languages, that were failing to generate sufficient revenue. An alarming new phenomenon appeared—the taxi-driving PhD, predecessor of today's avatar of educational disutility, the PhD on food stamps.[4]

In the face of so much class turmoil, young people rapidly rolled back their expectations to fit the narrowing career possibilities. UCLA's annual survey of undergraduate attitudes found a sharp decline in "altruism and social concerns," with a record 73 percent in 1987 reporting that their top goal was "being very well-off financially," compared with 39 percent in 1970.[5] I met them all the time on campuses, students who had started out with an interest in social work or environmentalism deciding regretfully to settle for majors in business or economics. But there was not much security even for the most practical-minded, because in the 1980s corporations also began to downsize (or "right-size") their white-collar workforces. GE was routinely culling out its bottom 15 percent of performers decades before Amazon got the idea. There were no more "jobs for life," no automatic promotions leading to a gold watch at retirement. Business gurus advised corporate employees to stop worrying about "who stole their cheese" and focus instead on "surfing the chaos."

But if you could not change the world or even chart your own career, you could still control your own body— what goes into it and how muscular energy is expended. Fitness pioneer Jim Fixx wrote in *The Complete Book of Running*, "Having lost faith in much of society, government, business, marriage, the church and so on—we seem to have turned to ourselves, putting what faith we can muster in our own minds and bodies."[6] He quoted one of his acolytes as saying that "running gives me a sense of controlling my own life,"[7] and I would say the same of working out: I may not be able to do much about grievous injustice in the world, at least not by myself or in very short order, but I can decide to increase the weight on the leg press machine by twenty pounds and achieve that within a few weeks. The gym, which once looked so alien and forbidding to me, became one of the few sites where I could reliably exert control.

To men of the left, like Lasch and Studs Terkel, who also piled on, fitness culture may have looked like a "retreat." But for women, "control over one's body" could be understood as a serious political goal. While you did not have to be a feminist to take up physical fitness, most women pouring into gyms had been through the punishing culture of female dieting and thinness, with its purging and fasts. They knew that women were supposed to focus on shrinking their bodies and becoming, as near as possible, invisible. To Gloria Steinem, this was another instance of patriarchal control; we were meant to be not only small, but weak, and to flout this expectation was in itself a form of feminist activism. "Yes," she wrote, "we need progress everywhere, but an increase in our physical strength could have more impact on the everyday lives of most women than the occasional role model in the boardroom or in the White House."[8]

Actor and activist Jane Fonda took up the challenge. She had been a victim of the misogynist thinness culture since the age of twelve, maintaining her startlingly lean body by self-induced vomiting up to twenty times a day. At some point in the 1980s, she realized she was in danger of destroying her esophagus with these constant acid rinses, later saying, "I had a career, I was winning awards, I was supporting nonprofits, I had a family. I had to make a choice: I live or I die."[9] Her recovery hinged on a new zeal for physical exercise in the form of aerobic dancing, which she took to marketing through the then-cutting-edge technology of videos. Millions of women danced along with her videos, reassured by the glamorous Fonda that they could be both sexy and strong. And clearly women had to be strong, since few families could hope to achieve middle-class status—marked by home ownership and private schools for the kids—without two working parents. The old financially dependent, stay-at-home mom was going out of style, although ironically she had far more time for exercise than her counterparts in the workforce.

But if women are in a way "masculinized" by the fitness culture, one might equally well say that men are "feminized" by it. Before the 1970s, only women were obsessed with their bodies, although in a morbid, anorectic way. But in the brightly lit gyms, where walls are typically lined by mirrors, both sexes are invited to inspect their body images for any unwanted bulges or loose bits of flesh and plan their workouts accordingly. Gay men flocked to the gyms, creating a highly chiseled standard of male beauty. The big change, though, was that heterosexual men were also "objectified" by the fitness culture, encouraged to see themselves as the objects of other people's appreciation—or, as the case may be, scorn. For both sexes in the endangered white-collar middle class, the body became an essential element of self-presentation, not just its size and general shape but the squareness of shoulders, the flatness of tummy, and, when sleeves were rolled up, the carefully sculpted contours of muscle.

Fitness, or the efforts to achieve it, quickly took on another function for the middle class—as an identifying signal or "class cue." Unfit behavior like smoking or reclining in front of the TV with a beer signified lower-class status, while a dedication to health, even if evidenced only by carrying a gym bag or yoga mat, advertised a loftier rank. Consider the matter of food choices. In the 1970s, foods seemed to sort themselves out along class lines, with the affluent opting for those deemed to be "natural," organic, whole grain or just "whole" (whatever a "whole food" is), and, above all, "pure." Intertwined between all these descriptors was the inescapable insistence on low-fat; that whole grain bread was not to be buttered. Jane Brody, the *New York Times* health columnist, relentlessly promoted the low-fat way of life to the masses, producing columns from the 1980s on with headlines like "Our Excessive Protein Intake Can Hurt Liver, Kidneys, Bone," "Carbohydrates Can Help You Lose Weight," and "'Chemicals' in Food Are Less Harmful Than Fat." Heeding her and other antifat fanatics like cardiologist Dean Ornish, Americans reduced their fat intake from 40 percent of calories ingested in 1970 to 34 percent in 2000,[10] with the result, which makes sense retrospectively, that we had an "obesity epidemic" as people gave up fat for "healthy" treats like fat-free cookies. But the long crusade against dietary fat succeeded in establishing that fat is for economic losers—an association prefigured by the word "grease," as in "greaser" or "greasy spoon."

Working out is another form of conspicuous consumption: Affluent people do it and, especially if muscular exertion is already part of their job, lower-class people tend to avoid it. There are exceptions like the working-class male body builders—"meatballs"—who can be found in places like Gold's Gym, as well as the lower-class women who attempt to shed pounds at Curves (a descendant of the women's-only gym where I started my workout career). By and large, though, working out is a reliable indicator of social status. Author and "sustainable living expert" Wanda Urbanska reported a conversation overheard between two women at a California gym, in which one complains about a new boyfriend, "The only thing wrong with him is he will not work out. He flat out refuses." To which her friend replies, "So you're going to have to let him go." "Do I have a choice?" the first woman responds.[11] The safest option for a single hoping to meet a partner who can pull his or her own weight is to restrict one's romantic interests to fellow health club members.

There is something almost utopian about the social spaces created by the fitness culture. Forget about the people who don't have the money or the time to participate. Ignore the low-paid janitors, maintenance workers, and front-desk clerks, whose jobs don't even offer health insurance. Just focus on the entitled inhabitants of the gym (or running or rowing group), who are encouraged to make themselves healthier and more attractive in a leisurely, carefully designed way, stopping for an occasional juice drink or chat. In this world, the sexes are more or less equal, people of all skin colors and sexual orientations mingle freely without the need to drink or dress up, bodies are displayed with a minimum of self-consciousness, there's free Wi-Fi and, in the locker rooms, free shampoo and moisturizer.

But stay around a little longer—thirty years of attending various gyms around the country in my case—and the picture looks a little less idyllic. Despite the pulsing pop music and comfortable clothes, gyms are not sites of spontaneity and play. There are rules beamed out from video monitors, mostly innocuous ones, like no cursing, "staring" at others, or expressing effort in audible form such as grunts or panting. Once, in a Key West gym, which you might imagine to be a somewhat permissive environment, I saw the manager chastise a young woman for moving too freely and rhythmically. "No dancing in the gym," he announced, nonsensically, as if to underscore the seriousness of our undertaking. A regimented dancelike experience, as in aerobics or Zumba, is fine, but unsupervised dance moves reek of hedonism, and working out is supposed to be a form of work. Most people come with a plan like "legs and shoulders today" or "45 minutes of cardio and 15 minutes of abs," usually preceded by a warm-up and topped off with several minutes of stretching on a mat.

Working out very much resembles work, or a curious blend of physical labor and office work. Members not only lift weights, for example, they often carry clipboards on which to record the number of reps and sets and the amount of weight lifted for each workout, like a supervisor monitoring a factory worker's performance. Even socializing is rare, if only because gym members are increasingly plugged into their iPods and can be alerted to an attempted communication (such as "May I work in?" or "Are you done with this now?") only by frantic waving and gestures.

The major interaction that goes on in gyms is not between members or between members and staff, but between the fitness devotee and his or her body. The body must be trained, disciplined, and put to ever more demanding tests, all administered and evaluated by the devotee's conscious mind. Compared to the mind, the body can be thought of as an animal, usually a domesticated or partially domesticated animal—capable of reflex and habit, though not of course conscious decision making. The poet Delmore Schwartz described his body as a "heavy bear.../ Breathing at my side, that heavy animal, / That heavy bear who sleeps with me."[12] We learn from coaches and fitness class instructors that, like any other beast of burden, the body is always inclined to take the path of least resistance unless we can "trick" it with a sudden variation in the workout routine. Western philosophy has long separated body from mind; fitness culture takes this dualism further—to an adversarial relationship in which mind struggles for control over the lazy, recalcitrant body. I plan to work out today, but I will not tell you exactly what I'll do, lest my body find out.

And why should the mind want to subdue the body systematically, repeatedly, day after day? Many gym-goers will tell you cheerfully that it makes them feel better, at least when the workout is over. But there's a darker, more menacing side to the preoccupation with fitness, and this is the widespread suspicion that if you can't control your own body, you're not fit, in any sense, to control anyone else, and in their work lives that is a large part of what typical gym-goers do. We are talking here about a relative elite of people who are more likely to give orders than to take them— managers and professionals. In this class, there are steep penalties for being overweight or in any other way apparently unhealthy. Flabby people are less likely to be hired or promoted;[13] they may even be reprimanded and obliged to undergo the company's "wellness" program, probably consisting of exercise (on- or off-site), nutritional counseling to promote weight loss, and, if indicated, lessons in smoking cessation.

Employee wellness is not a traditional concern of large capitalist enterprises, which are historically better known for imposing unhealthy conditions on their workers— exposure to hazardous substances in the case of blue-collar workers, punishing workloads and unholy levels of stress for workers of all collar colors. At some point in the 1970s and '80s, though, companies got the idea that promoting individual health might reduce their expenditures on employee health insurance, an insight that eventually led to what is now a $6 billion industry in creating and managing corporate wellness programs. Participation in these is not entirely optional. Some employers will raise workers' contributions to their health insurance by $500 or so and then "waive" the price increase for employees who undergo a health assessment and submit to the follow-up regimen, typically involving weight loss goals. Many workers complain—at least to outside researchers—that corporate wellness programs are coercive and overly intrusive, just one more source of workplace-related stress.[14] Promoters of corporate wellness programs claim that they reduce employer health insurance expenditures by a hefty percentage, but a massive 2014 study by the Rand Corporation found that they have "little if any immediate effects on the amount employers spend on health care."[15]

It was the existence of widespread health insurance that turned fitness into a moral imperative. Insurance involves risk sharing, with those in need of care being indirectly subsidized by those who are healthier, so that if you are sick, or overweight, or just guilty of insufficient attention to personal wellness, you are a drag on your company, if not your nation. As the famed physician and Rockefeller Foundation president John H. Knowles put it in 1977:

> The cost of sloth, gluttony, alcoholic intemperance, reckless driving, sexual frenzy, and smoking is now a national, and not an individual, responsibility.... One man's freedom in health is another man's shackle in taxes and insurance premiums.[16]

Or, in the words of former secretary of Health, Education, and Welfare Joseph Califano, "We have met the enemy and they are us."[17] Never mind that poverty, race, and occupation play a huge role in determining one's health status, the doctrine of individual responsibility means that the less-than-fit person is a suitable source not only of revulsion but resentment. The objection raised over and over to any proposed expansion of health insurance was, in so many words: Why should I contribute to the care of those degenerates who choose to smoke and eat cheeseburgers?

The idea that we are each individually responsible for our own health is perhaps most significant for what it omits: not only environmental and socioeconomic factors, but doctors and health care providers of all sorts, who were by and large unprepared for the fitness revolution. A 2014 "white paper" from the Bipartisan Policy Center reported that 75 percent of US physicians felt that their medical training in nutrition and exercise was insufficient for counseling patients with obesity-related problems.[18] In fact, doctors and fitness gurus seem to occupy non-overlapping worlds. You will often find, stamped in small letters on fitness equipment, the advice that you not undertake a fitness program without first "obtaining a physical examination," but of course an exam is not required for gym membership, nor are you likely to find posters in gyms reminding you of the need for medical screenings. Similarly doctors' offices do not, at least in my experience, offer literature or advice on exercise programs, nor do they encourage clients to be environmentally responsible. A doctor may inquire as to whether you "exercise," but in most cases he or she is satisfied with a simple "yes." The exception is the rare celebrity doctor, like the scientifically discredited "Dr. Oz,"[19] who ministers to millions of TV viewers at a time, offering a mix of nutritional and exercise tips along with alternative and "natural" remedies such as aromatherapy and mud baths.

Besides, the fitness movement's core ideology of self-improvement and self-responsibility tends to render physicians irrelevant. Why ask a possibly flaccid medical doctor for diet and exercise tips that you can readily find on TV or the Internet? Why waste precious time sitting in a doctor's waiting room when you could be working out? Jerry Rubin credited yuppies—that being the identity he embraced after growing out of the Yippies—with bringing about "America's health revolution," explaining that "yuppies don't wait to get sick and then let a doctor do the rest with pills and surgery; they work to avoid getting sick in the first place. From this has emerged the nation's new awareness of self-responsibility for fitness and nutrition."[20]

One way for the medical profession to maintain its grip in a world of increasingly do-it-yourself health care was to establish the doctor's office as a kind of way station along the patient's "fitness journey," a place to check in periodically on one's blood pressure, cholesterol levels, and other markers of fitness success. And for years in the 1980s and '90s, fitness devotees were content with this arrangement, carefully managing their diets and exercise regimens, and reporting to the physician now and then for a pat on the back. But then, almost without warning, the job of monitoring people's health underwent a sudden burst of automation. There had always been a degree of self-monitoring—weighing oneself and, in the case of diabetics, checking blood sugar levels throughout the day. In the twenty-first century, technologies arose to enable continuous, convenient, unobtrusive self-monitoring of dozens of variables, including blood pressure, heart rate, calorie intake, number of steps taken in a day, even mood. Epileptics can wear devices that will warn them of oncoming seizures; asthmatics can be alerted to incipient attacks. In 2014, *Forbes* reported that the market for devices was "red hot,"[21] and indeed, a year later, that one-third of American consumers were using at least some kind of wearable health monitoring device.[22]

The medical profession was no more prepared for self-monitoring than it had been for the fitness revolution. Most frontline practitioners were still reeling from the challenge of electronic medical record-keeping, and that only dealt with data a doctor could collect—not the potentially unlimited streams of data patients could now gather for themselves. One reaction was to denounce the self-monitoring devices as mere "toys," not FDA-approved or accurate enough to base medical decision making on. More churlishly, some doctors accused the devices of fostering hypochondria, as patients became obsessed with insignificant fluctuations in their biodata. When the health-obsessed computer scientist Ray Kurzweil first attempted to engage a physician in his ultra-detailed concerns, he was cut off by the doctor, who said, "Look, I just don't have time for this; I have patients who are dying that I have to attend to."[23]

Other physicians were more welcoming—most notably Eric Topol, the cardiologist, geneticist, and self-monitoring innovator who was declared one of the "rock stars of science" by *GQ* magazine in 2009.[24] Declaring that the self-monitoring movement was the "biggest shake-up in the history of medicine," he announced that the new role of the physician was to prescribe not drugs or surgery, but self-monitoring apps. "You name the condition, we get the apps to match up with your phone," he told the BBC.[25] And physicians could still play a role in helping the patient interpret the volumes of unrelated data that his or her devices were collecting; unless of course that function is also automated. Already, a swarm of new start-ups is developing "aggregator platforms" that will integrate the various data flowing in from wearable devices, potentially leaving the doctor almost entirely out of the loop.

But for the average seeker of health and fitness, like myself, whose self-monitoring has probably not advanced beyond the Fitbit (which counts the number of steps you take each day) stage, it hardly matters whether physicians endorse or condemn the new technologies. We have our own goals and quotas to fulfill—number of stairs to climb on the StairMaster, reps to perform with ten- or twenty-pound weights, minutes to travel on the inclined treadmill—and in these endeavors we are far more likely to be influenced by fitness websites, personal trainers, and other gym-goers than by any sort of health care professional. In fact, in the ultimate concession to the DIY trend, growing numbers of physicians now employ nutrition and fitness "coaches," who, like personal trainers in gyms, will patiently attend to the minutiae of one's self-care,[26] leaving the doctor to scan the horizon for oncoming threats.

It's tempting to invest one's daily workout with a kind of dwarfish heroism. It may look like I'm just doggedly repeating the same routine with slight variations from day to day, but the real drama lies in the invisible confrontation between mind and muscle, in which I am the only conscious participant. Can I increase the load on my quads, and by how much? Are the lats getting a little lazy, and what will it take to shake them up? In the course of my own fitness "journey" I have gone from being an embarrassed weakling to something of a show-off—taking over a machine from a young, strong man and ostentatiously increasing the weight on it, preferably while he is still watching. At my zenith, I could draw spectators for my leg presses at 270 pounds and lunges while holding a twenty-pound weight in each hand. None of this has had much effect on my daily life, other than to make me cackle contemptuously when a supermarket clerk asks if I need help getting my groceries to the car.

Then, in just the last few years, I began to hit a wall. I developed temporarily disabling knee problems, which X-rays showed were attributable to overexertion rather than, as was to be expected at my age, arthritis. My lower back easily clenched into knots. I had to try to develop a less adversarial stance toward my body, or at least learn how to "listen" to it. I adjusted my routine accordingly and expanded my menu of stretches. The ideology of fitness, which had so far encouraged me to treat my body as a recalcitrant mass I was required to carry around with me everywhere, showed a softer side, emphasizing the "wisdom of the body" and the need to develop some sort of détente with it. For a moment I even toyed with the idea of a yoga class, possibly including meditation, before deciding that I'm not quite old enough for that.

If anything, the culture of fitness has grown more combative than when I first got involved. It is no longer enough to "have a good workout," as the receptionist at the gym advises every day; you should "crush your workout." Health and strength are tedious goals compared to my gym's new theme of "explosive strength," achieved, as far as I can see, through repeated whole-body swinging of a kettlebell. If your gym isn't sufficiently challenging, you might want to try an "ultra-extreme warrior workout"[27] or buy a "home fitness system" from P90X, which recently tweeted a poster of an ultra-cut male upper body, head bowed as if in prayer, with the caption "A moment of silence please, for my body has no idea what I'm about to put it through."[28] Or you could join CrossFit, the fastest-growing type of gym in the world and also allegedly the most physically punishing. "We have sought to build a program that will best prepare trainees for any physical contingency," the company boasts, "not only for the unknown, but for the unknowable,"[29] and the latter category includes the zombie apocalypse.[30] The mind's struggle for mastery over the body has become a kind of mortal combat.

The South African runner Oscar Pistorius, who is now serving a sentence for the 2013 murder of his girlfriend, had more to overcome than most athletes: His legs had been amputated below the knees when he was a toddler. But he managed to become both a Paralympic and Olympic champion. Tattooed on his back is a modified verse from Corinthians:

> I do not run like a man running aimlessly
> I do not fight like a man beating the air;
> I execute each stride with intent;
> I beat my body and make it my slave
> I bring it under my complete subjection...[31]

CHAPTER FIVE

The Madness of Mindfulness

In the struggle between mind and body, perpetually reenacted by fitness-seekers, the mind is almost universally conceived as the "good guy"—the moral overdog that must by all rights prevail. Contemporary fitness culture concedes a certain advisory status to the body: We should "listen" to it, since, after all, the body is capable of doing a great many important things on its own, from healing wounds to incubating fetuses, with no discernible instructions from the conscious mind. So if your hamstrings are squealing with pain, it may be time to recalibrate the leg lifts and squats. All-purpose guru Deepak Chopra advises:

> *Be open to your body.* It's always speaking. Be willing to listen. *Trust your body.* Every cell is on your side, which means you have hundreds of billions of allies.[1]

It's up to you, of course, to tune in to the body or ignore it. As a health columnist puts it:

Your body pays attention to you. It thinks you're important! If you've spent a whole lot of time ignoring how you
feel, just bulldozing along—your body has probably decided you're not interested in listening to these lines of
communication. It hits the mute button. That's OK, you
can turn your volume back on.[2]

The superiority of mind over body, or, more majestically,
spirit over matter, is inscribed in every post-pagan religion
and philosophical system. In the Manichean religion of
third-century-CE Mesopotamia—which drew on Christian Gnosticism as well as Buddhism—all of cosmology is
a "struggle between a good, spiritual world of light, and
an evil, material world of darkness,"[3] a theme that came
to full, dark flower in the medieval Catholic Church, with
its celebration of self-mortification—saints, for example,
who dined on little more than the dust they found in their
monastic cells. To achieve spiritual salvation, the spirit had
to be freed from the body and all its vile inclinations, including its tendency toward disease and corruption. Today's
Christianity, Islam, and Judaism, while far more permissive,
often require adherence to some dietary rules and physical
acts of obeisance like kneeling and prostration in prayer or
wearing restrictive clothing. At the very least, the mind or
spirit is expected to keep a tight rein on the body's sloth-
ful, gluttonous, and lustful impulses. A twentieth-century
anorectic associated her wasted body with "absolute purity,
hyperintellectuality and transcendence of the flesh," adding
that "my soul seemed to grow as my body waned."[4]

But can the mind be trusted? Surveying today's fitness

culture, a mid-twentieth-century psychiatrist would no doubt find reasons to suspect a variety of mental disorders—masochism, narcissism, obsessive-compulsive disorder, and homoerotic tendencies (which were viewed as pathological until the 1970s)—any of which could indicate the need for professional intervention. Even the untrained eye can detect the occasional skeletal anorectic in the gym, sweating through hours of cardiovascular training, and start to question the assumed intellectual superiority of the mind. We have come, hesitantly, to respect the "wisdom of the body," but can we be sure of the wisdom of the mind?

Just within the last decade, a new reason for alarm has arisen. Not only may the mind be twisted by the traditional emotional disorders like depression, but its fundamental cognitive powers appear to be dwindling. Teachers, parents, and psychologists have noted a steep decline in the ability to pay attention, among both children and adults. A 2015 study found that the average adult attention span had shrunk from twelve seconds a dozen years ago to eight seconds, which is shorter than the attention span of a goldfish.[5] Something seems to be going very wrong with the human mind, not in its emotional responses to the world, which have always been a bit unreliable, but in its ability to perceive and understand that world. Among the many diagnoses being bandied about are autism, which now occupies an entire "spectrum" of symptoms, Asperger's syndrome, attention deficit disorder (ADD), and attention deficit hyperactivity disorder (ADHD)—all of which overlap in symptomatology and can markedly affect academic performance. Any parent whose child was performing less than brilliantly in school would be remiss not to seek medical help.

ADD and ADHD are now the most common pediatric diagnoses after asthma, partly for reasons that have nothing to do with any actual epidemiology. In the first decade of the twenty-first century, drug companies started marketing stimulants like Adderall and Ritalin as treatments for ADD/ADHD, often targeting parents and even children directly. One such ad showed a mother hugging a little boy who has gotten a B+ on a test, captioned with "Finally, schoolwork which matches his intelligence."[6] Another showed a kid in a monster costume removing his monster-head-covering to reveal a smiling blond boy. "There's a great kid in there," reads the text. "Now there's a new way to help him out."[7] Whether the drugs worked or not to boost grades, affluent parents were discovering that a diagnosis of ADD/ADHD could warrant giving their child additional time to complete in-class tests—a small but possibly decisive advantage in the competition to get into a good high school or college.

It did not take years of laboratory research to get to the likely source of this new "epidemic." Parents could see what was happening to their own children, who were being drawn to electronic devices—cell phones, computers, and iPads—as if to opium-infused cupcakes. They stare at the small screens for hours a day, often switching moment by moment between games, videos, and texting their friends. They have trouble focusing on homework or anything else in "the real world" even when their devices are forcibly removed. Neuroscientists confirmed that electronic addiction was "rewiring" the human brain, depleting attention span[8] and degrading the quality of sleep.[9] In fact, as they withdrew from the physical world into their texts and their tweets, adults could see the same things happening to themselves. The term "distracted parenting" was invented to describe the parent who could barely focus on his or her children anymore, certainly not to the degree required to enforce a few hours of abstinence from devices a day. And what good could a parent do when the schools themselves increasingly use laptops and iPads as instruments of learning? The small screens seemed to have swallowed the world.

The Technological Fix

The perpetrator was easy enough to locate—in Silicon Valley or, more generally, the high-tech industry that created the tempting devices and social networks that consume so much of our time. Silicon Valley is not just the source of the problem; it also seemed to be ground zero of the inattentiveness epidemic. A 2001 article in *Wired* sounded an early alarm: Diagnoses of autism and Asperger's syndrome were skyrocketing in Santa Clara County, home of Silicon Valley.[10] Among the adult population of the Valley, surely something was wrong with Steve Jobs, who alternated between obsessive attention to details and complete withdrawal into himself, between a spiritual aloofness and uncontrolled temper tantrums. Some observers thought they detected a hint of autism in the unblinking, almost affect-free Bill Gates, and the characters in HBO's *Silicon Valley* are portrayed as well "within the spectrum." There is even a "Silicon Valley syndrome," defined, incoherently, by the crowdsourced Urban Dictionary as "a collection of personality traits and physical characteristics specific to individuals residing around the San Francisco Bay Area. The effects of SVS are often confused for autism or Helen Keller [*sic*]."[11] Put that together with Apple's slogan "Think different," and you might conclude that Silicon Valley has a problem not only with grammar, but with thinking itself.

Rising concerns about shrinking attention spans should—if anyone had been paying attention—have created a sense of crisis in Silicon Valley. Suppose the company manufacturing a nutritional supplement advertised as "miraculous" was confronted with claims that its product actually enfeebles its users—which was roughly the situation the tech industry found itself in. Not only did Silicon Valley's corporate culture encourage a "syndrome" of inattentiveness and self-involvement, but its products seem to spread the same derangement to everyone else. The devices that were supposed to make us smarter and more connected to other humans were actually messing with our minds, causing "Net brain" and "monkey mind," as well as physical disorders associated with long hours of sitting. As we click between Twitter and Facebook, text and hypertext, one link and another, synapses are being formed and then broken with febrile inconstancy—or so the neuroscientists warn us—leaving the neuronal scaffolding too fragile to house large thoughts. Hence the emergence of "digital detox camps" where grown-ups pay to live without electronic devices—as well as alcohol, sex, and gluten—in order to "reconnect" with the real world.[12]

A less arrogant industry might have settled for warning labels on its phones and pads—"Do not use while driving or attempting to hold a conversation," for example. But Silicon Valley "has an arrogance problem," tech columnist Farhad Manjoo announced in the *Wall Street Journal* in 2013, in response to a tech titan's plea for greater independence from regulation:

> For Silicon Valley's own sake, the triumphalist tone needs to be kept in check. Everyone knows that Silicon Valley aims to take over the world. But if they want to succeed, the Valley's inhabitants would be wise to at least pretend to be more humble in their approach.[13]

But humility was not in Silicon Valley's repertoire. Had they not, in just a couple of decades, transformed—or to use their current favorite verb, "disrupted"—the worlds of entertainment, communications, business, shopping, dating, and just about everything else? In the process, at least fourteen billionaires had emerged in the Valley itself, which is certainly an undercount of tech billionaires nationwide. Wall Street and Hollywood could generate centi-millionaires; only in Silicon Valley could a young man (and it is almost always a man) without a college degree rather suddenly acquire an eight-figure fortune. Silicon Valley, whether in the Bay Area, Austin, Cambridge, or New York's Silicon Alley, is a setting that breeds megalomania or, as tech critic Evgeny Morozov terms it, "'solutionism': an intellectual pathology that recognizes problems as problems based on just one criterion: whether they are 'solvable' with a nice and clean technological solution at our disposal."[14]

Anything is possible, any problem solvable, with a simple "hack." Space travel? PayPal cofounder Elon Musk now heads up SpaceX, the first private space travel company. Health? Silicon Valley generates the personal monitoring devices that can continually reveal your inner workings far better than a doctor's office could. Who needs a doctor anyway? Picking up on the evidence-based critiques of medical practice, Vinod Khosla, "one of Silicon Valley's most revered venture capitalists," publicly announced that "healthcare is like witchcraft and just based on tradition" rather than being driven by data.[15]

Far better to pick up a little biochemistry and proceed to "biohack" your own body. Dave Asprey describes himself as "a young, brand-new multimillionaire entrepreneur" when he confronted his own obesity and attempted, unsuccessfully, to cure it by dieting and doing a ninety-minute workout per day. Then he realized that

> our bodies and the Internet are not all that different. They are both complex systems with big pieces of data that are missing, misunderstood or hidden. When I looked at my body that way, I realized that I could learn to hack my biology using the same techniques I used to hack computer systems and the Internet.[16]

Asprey's lifesaving hack turned out to be "Bulletproof Coffee"—expensive mold-free coffee containing a generous portion of melted butter—which he now markets online and through his cafés. Exercise turned out to be just too time-consuming.

For obsessive biohacking no one tops Ray Kurzweil, the futurist, inventor, and bestselling author of a book on the coming "singularity," when artificial intelligence will become self-improving and overtake the human mind. Like Asprey, Kurzweil sees the body as a machine—in fact a computer—that can be continually upgraded. "I have a personal program to combat each of the degenerative disease and aging processes," he writes. "My view is that I am *reprogramming my biochemistry* in the same way I reprogram the computers in my life."[17] The only exercise he undertakes is walking, and his nutritional routine would seem not to leave time for workouts in a gym. Every day he takes "about 250" pills containing nutritional supplements, on top of which he spends a day a week at a clinic where supplements are delivered right into his bloodstream. "Every few months," he relates, "I test dozens of levels of nutrients (such as vitamins, minerals, and fats), hormones and metabolic by-products in my blood."[18]

The goal here is not something as mundane as health. Silicon Valley's towering hubris demands nothing less than immortality. The reason why Kurzweil has transformed himself into a walking chemistry lab is to prolong his life just long enough for the next set of biomedical breakthroughs to come along, say in 2040, after which we'll be able to load our bodies with millions of nanobots programmed to fight disease. One way or another, other tech titans aim to achieve the same thing. As *Newsweek* reports:

Peter Thiel, the billionaire co-founder of PayPal, plans to live to be 120. Compared with some other tech billionaires, he doesn't seem particularly ambitious. Dmitry Itskov, the "godfather" of the Russian Internet, says his goal is to live to 10,000; Larry Ellison, co-founder of Oracle, finds the notion of accepting mortality "incomprehensible," and Sergey Brin, co-founder of Google, hopes to someday "cure death."[19]

There is, to say the least, a profound sense of entitlement here. Oracle's Larry Ellison is reportedly "used to getting his way, and he doesn't see why that should ever stop. 'Death makes me very angry,' he has said, explaining why he has spent hundreds of millions to fund antiaging research."[20] If you are one of the richest men in the world, and presumably, since this is Silicon Valley, one of the smartest, why should you ever die?

Controlling Your Mind

With immortality on the agenda, surely the little matter of mass inattentiveness had a solution, and I mean a "solution" in the "solutionist" sense—something convenient, marketable, and preferably available on existing devices. But the solution, when it made its way to Silicon Valley, came from a realm apparently unrelated to digital technology, and that is religion—in this case, Buddhism. Jon Kabat-Zinn, a Zen-trained psychologist in Cambridge, Massachusetts, had already extracted what he took as the secularized core of Buddhism and termed it "mindfulness," which he extolled in two bestsellers in the late 1990s. I first heard the word in 1998 from a wealthy landlady in Berkeley, who advised me to be "mindful" of the suffocating Martha Stewart–ish décor of the apartment I was renting from her, which of course I was doing everything possible to unsee. The probable connection to Buddhism emerged when I had to turn to a tenants' rights group to collect my security deposit. People like me—renters?—she responded in an angry letter, were oppressing Tibetans and disrespected the Dalai Lama.

During the same stint in the Bay Area, I learned that rich locals liked to unwind at Buddhist monasteries in the hills where, for a few thousand dollars, they could spend a weekend doing manual labor for the monks. Buddhism, or some adaptation thereof, was becoming a class signifier, among Caucasians anyway, and nowhere was it more ostentatious than Silicon Valley, where star player Steve Jobs had been a Buddhist or perhaps a Hindu—he seems not to have made a distinction—even before it was fashionable for CEOs to claim a spiritual life. Guided by an in-house Buddhist, Google started offering its "Search Inside Yourself" trainings, promoting attention and self-knowledge, in 2007.

Mindfulness went public as a kind of "movement" only in the second decade of the twenty-first century, though, when Soren Gordhamer, a former teacher of meditation to at-risk youth and at one point an aide to Hollywood's chief Buddhist, Richard Gere, found himself broke, divorced, and in the grip of a terrible Twitter addiction. Something had to be done to counter the addiction to devices, and it had to be something that in no way threatened the billionaires who had lured us into it. As *Mindful* magazine later pointed out:

> The lords and leaders of high tech aren't about to dismiss new technology as the beginning of the end of humankind—not only because they don't want to work against their own economic interests, but because they believe in the innovative, interactive world fostered by new technologies.... Yet they also know that technology can be distracting, not only from where we are in any given moment but from where we ought to be going.[21]

In a stroke of genius, Gordhamer found a way to raise the issue while actually flattering the tech titans. He claims to have discovered that, while the rest of us struggle with intractable distraction, leaders from Google, LinkedIn, Twitter, and other major tech companies seem to be "tapped into an inner dimension that guides their work."[22] He called it "wisdom" and started a series of annual conferences called Wisdom 2.0, based originally in San Francisco, in which corporate leaders, accompanied by celebrity gurus, could share the source of their remarkable serenity, which was soon known as mindfulness.

At the same time, in London, a former Buddhist monk with a degree in Circus Arts, Andy Puddicombe, was trying to figure out how to spread Buddhist meditation techniques within the generally religion-averse business class. He and a partner created a company called Headspace, which at first

staged events where large groups of people paid to participate in guided meditation sessions. When the customers de-
manded more convenient ways of packaging the experience,
Headspace started marketing CDs, podcasts, and eventually
a cell-phone-accessible app, distributed by Apple and An-
droid. Politically and monetarily, this was another stroke of
genius. It catapulted Puddicombe from near destitution to a
net worth of £25 million,[23] while, through efforts like Wisdom 2.0, simultaneously transforming the tech titans from
being the villains in the inattentiveness epidemic to the putative saviors. There was an "irony," *Fast Company* noted,
"in using technology to deliver mindfulness coaching to a
population that's more and more tech-frazzled."[24] Bestselling psychologist Daniel Goleman observed, more bluntly,
"What a clever way to make money: Create a problem you
can then solve."[25]

Mass-market mindfulness began to roll out of the Bay
Area like a brand-new app. Very much like an app, in fact,
or a whole swarm of apps. There are over five hundred
mindfulness apps available, bearing names like "Simply
Being" and "Buddhify." Previous self-improvement trends
were transmitted via books, inspirational speakers, and
CDs; mindfulness can be carried around on a smart-
phone. Most of these apps feature timed stretches of
meditation, some as brief as one minute, accompanied by
soothing voices, soporific music, and cloying images of
forests and waterfalls.

This is Buddhism sliced up, commodified, and drained
of all reference to the transcendent. In case the connection
to the tech industry is unclear, a Silicon Valley venture cap-

italist blurbed a seminal mindfulness manual by calling it "the instruction manual that should come with our iPhones and Blackberries."[26] You might think that the actual Buddha had devoted his time sitting under the Bodhi tree to product testing; the word "enlightenment" never arises in the mindfulness lexicon.

Today mindfulness, in its sleek and secular form, has spread far beyond Silicon Valley and its signature industry, becoming just another numbingly ubiquitous feature of the verbal landscape, as "positive thinking" once was. While an earlier, more arduous version of Buddhism attracted few celebrities other than Richard Gere, mindfulness boasts a host of prominent practitioners—Arianna Huffington, Gwyneth Paltrow, and Anderson Cooper among them. It debuted at Davos in 2013 to an overflow crowd, and Wisdom 2.0 conferences have taken place in New York and Dublin as well as San Francisco, with attendees often fanning out to become missionaries for the new mind-set—starting their own coaching businesses or designing their own apps. A recent Wisdom 2.0 event in San Francisco advertised speeches by corporate representatives of Starbucks and Eileen Fisher as well as familiar faces from Google and Facebook. Aetna health insurance offers its thirty-four thousand employees a twelve-week program and dreams of expanding to include all its customers, who will presumably be made healthier by clearing their minds. Even General Mills, which dates back to the nineteenth century, has added meditation rooms to its buildings, finding that a seven-week course produces striking results:

[Eighty-three] per cent of participants said they were "taking time each day to optimise my personal productivity"—
up from 23 per cent before the course. Eighty-two per
cent said they now make time to eliminate tasks with limited productivity value—up from 32 per cent before the
course.[27]

It was Silicon Valley, though, that legitimized mindfulness for the rest of the business world. If mindfulness had
first taken root in General Mills, it would never have gained
the status it's acquired from Google and Facebook; baking
products just don't have the cachet of digital devices. Silicon Valley is, after all, the "innovation center of the universe," according to its boosters, home of the "best and the
brightest," along with the new "masters of the universe"
who replaced the old ones after the financial crash that temporarily humbled Wall Street. Mindfulness may have roots
in an ancient religion, but the Valley's imprimatur established that it was rational, scientific, and forward-looking.

To the tech industry, the great advantage of mindfulness
is that it seemed to be based firmly on science; no "hippie
bullshit" or other "woo-woo" was involved. Positive thinking had never gained much traction in Silicon Valley, possibly because the tech titans needed no help in believing that
they could do (or hack or disrupt) anything they set out to
do. The other problem with positive thinking is that despite
the efforts of PhD-level "positive psychologists," it had no
clear scientific backing and in fact bore a strong resemblance to "magical thinking"—"If I think it, it must be so."
But advocates of mindfulness could always point to a 2004

study by a neuroscientist showing that Buddhist monks with about ten thousand hours of meditation under their belts had altered patterns of brain activity.[28] Shorter bouts of meditation seemed to work at least temporary changes in novices. The field of "contemplative neuroscience" was born, and Silicon Valley seized on it for a much-needed "neural hack." Through meditation, monastic or app-guided, anyone could reach directly into their own moist brain tissue and "resculpt" it in a calmer, more attentive direction. Mindfulness, as its promoters put it, fosters—or as it is often put, even "induces"—"neuroplasticity."

"Neuroplasticity" is an impressively scientific-sounding term, but it is an innate property of neuronal tissue, which persists whether we make a conscious effort to rewire our brains or not. Everything we experience subjectively, every thought and emotion, produces at least transient physiological changes in the brain. Trauma and addiction can lead to longer-lasting changes; even fleeting events may leave the chemical traces in the brain that we experience as memory. In fact, "plasticity" is a pallid descriptor for the constant, ongoing transformation of brain tissue: Neurons reach out to each other through tiny membranous protrusions called "spines," which can form or disappear within minutes or seconds. Spines appear to be involved in the formation of new synapses linking neurons, which in turn hold together the ever-changing structure of neural firing patterns. Synapses that fire frequently grow stronger, while the inactive ones wither. Well-connected neurons thrive while neglected ones die. There is even some evidence that neurons in mature animals can reproduce.

What there is no evidence for, however, is any particularly salubrious effect of meditation, especially in byte-sized doses. This was established through a mammoth federally sponsored "meta-analysis" of existing studies, published in 2014, which found that meditation programs can help treat stress-related symptoms, but that they are no more effective in doing so than other interventions, such as muscle relaxation, medication, or psychotherapy.[29] There is no excuse for ignoring this study, which achieved worldwide attention. So maybe meditation does have a calming, "centering" effect, but so does an hour of concentration on a math problem or a glass of wine with friends. I personally recommend a few hours a day with small children or babies, who can easily charm anyone into entering their alternative universe. As for Silicon Valley's unique contribution, mindfulness apps, a recent study concluded that there is

> an almost complete lack of evidence supporting the usefulness of those applications. We found no randomized clinical trials evaluating the impact of these applications on mindfulness training or health indicators, and the potential for mobile mindfulness applications remains largely unexplored.[30]

For an industry based on empirical science and employing large numbers of engineers, Silicon Valley has been remarkably incurious about the scientific basis of mindfulness—probably because the "neuroplasticity" concept is just too alluring. The line of reasoning—or, I should say, analogizing—goes like this: If the brain can be resculpted through conscious effort, then mindfulness is as imperative as physical exercise; the brain is a "muscle," and, like any muscle, in need of training. The metaphor of mind-as-muscle is almost ubiquitous in the mindfulness industry. For example, one popular and highly rated mindfulness app, called "Get Some Headspace," advertises itself as a "gym membership for the mind." Google's chief motivator, Chade-Meng Tan, whose official corporate title was "Jolly Good Fellow," installed the company's mindfulness training program, "Search Inside Yourself," in 2007, later telling the *Guardian*:

> If you are a company leader who says employees should be encouraged to exercise, nobody looks at you funny.... The same thing is happening to meditation and mindfulness, because now that it's become scientific, it has been demystified. It's going to be seen as fitness for the mind.[31]

So it's not "science" that legitimates mindfulness practice. The only thing that science contributed was the notion of neuroplasticity, which morphed into the mind-as-muscle metaphor, which in turn suggested the metaphor of mindfulness as a form of fitness training. The mind can be controlled much as the body can—through disciplined exercise, possibly conducted in a special space, like a corporate meditation room, which, Tan suggests, should be seen as no more outré than the company gym.

Of course, there is a slight metaphysical mystery here: Who is in charge? In the physical fitness case, the duality lies only between the body, which was thought to be inert, and the mind, imagined as an immaterial essence—the site of "I" or "us." But if the mind has also been reduced to a substance, though fortunately a malleable one that can be molded and controlled, then where is the "I"? This is one of the paradoxes of the endeavor to use the mind, conceived as a conscious agent, to control itself. Ruby Wax, a high-profile British mindfulness teacher and promoter, seems to hint at the problem when she says:

> The difficult thing is, your brain can't tell there's something wrong with your brain. If you have a rash on your leg, you can look down and see it. But you don't have a spare brain to make an assessment of your own brain. You're always the last to know—that's the bitch.[32]

But whichever prevails in the mind-body duality, the hope, the goal—the cherished assumption—is that by working together, the mind and the body can act as a perfectly self-regulating machine. Certainly the body had seemed willing to cooperate ever since the 1932 publication of physiologist Walter B. Cannon's book *The Wisdom of the Body*, which laid out the delicate mechanisms of homeostasis, through which the body attempts to keep blood sugar level, acid/base balance, and body temperature at constant "normal" levels. Now add in the brain, with its ability to send the individual mind ranging out into the collective mind represented by books, experts, and the Internet—bringing back important new information: Eat more vegetables (or turmeric, or whatever is fashionable at the moment); exercise daily; take time to unwind. Combine mind plus body with freshly updated data, some of it perhaps collected on your self-monitoring devices, and act quickly to generate fresh instructions to forestall any looming problems. This, I imagine, is how Silicon Valley "immortalists" spend their time—scanning all the health-related information and instantly applying it—which may seem a small price to pay for eternal life.

CHAPTER SIX

Death in Social Context

Many of the people who got caught up in the health "craze" of the late twentieth century—people who exercised, watched what they ate, abstained from smoking and heavy drinking—have nevertheless died. Lucille Roberts, owner of the chain of women's gyms that introduced me to the fitness culture, died incongruously from lung cancer at the age of fifty-nine, even though she was a "self-described exercise nut" who, the *New York Times* reported, "wouldn't touch a French fry, much less smoke a cigarette."[1] Jerry Rubin, who devoted his later years to trying every supposedly health-promoting diet fad, therapy, and meditation system he could find, jaywalked into Wilshire Boulevard at the age of fifty-six and died of his injuries two weeks later. If this trend were to continue, everyone who participated in the fitness culture—as well as everyone who sat it out—will at some point be dead.

Some of these deaths were genuinely shocking. Jerome Rodale, the founder of *Prevention* magazine and an early promoter of organic food, died of a heart attack at age seventy-two, while taping *The Dick Cavett Show*—a death made particularly memorable by Rodale's off-camera statement that he had "decided to live to be a hundred."[2] Jim Fixx, author of the bestselling *The Complete Book of Running*, believed he could outwit the cardiac problems that had carried his father off to an early death by running at least ten miles a day and restricting himself to a diet consisting mostly of pasta, salads, and fruit. But he was found dead on the side of a Vermont road in 1984, at the age of only fifty-two. In 2017, Henry S. Lodge, coauthor of the bestselling *Younger Next Year: Live Strong, Fit, and Sexy—Until You're 80 and Beyond*, died of pancreatic cancer at the still-youthful age of fifty-eight. In an obituary, his coauthor Chris Crowley wrote:

> I suppose the question may arise: doesn't his premature death undercut the premise of the book? No, not for one minute. We always said that the life-style we were promoting—and which Harry followed carefully—would reduce the risk of death from cancers and heart disease, among other things, by half, but not entirely. You could catch a lousy break, "ski into a tree" or "grow a tangerine in your brain pan," as [our] book puts it.[3]

Even more disturbing, to those who knew about it, was the untimely demise of John H. Knowles, director of the Rockefeller Foundation and promulgator of what became known as the "doctrine of personal responsibility" for one's health. Most illnesses are self-inflicted, he argued—the result of "gluttony, alcoholic intemperance, reckless driving, sexual frenzy, and smoking,"[4] as well as other bad choices. The "idea of a 'right' to health," he wrote, "should be replaced by the idea of an individual moral obligation to preserve one's own health." But he died of pancreatic cancer at the age of fifty-two, prompting one physician commentator to observe that "clearly we can't always be held responsible for our health."[5]

Still, we persist in subjecting anyone who dies at a seemingly untimely age to a kind of bio-moral autopsy: Did she smoke? Drink excessively? Eat too much fat and not enough fiber? Can she, in other words, be blamed for her own death? When two British entertainers, David Bowie and Alan Rickman, both died in early 2016 of what major US newspapers described only as "cancer," some readers complained that it is the responsibility of obituaries to reveal what kind of cancer.[6] Ostensibly this information would help promote "awareness" of the particular cancers involved, as Betty Ford's openness about her breast cancer diagnosis helped to destigmatize that disease. It would also, of course, prompt judgments about the victim's "lifestyle." Would David Bowie have died—at, we should note, the quite respectable age of sixty-nine—if he hadn't been a smoker?

Apple cofounder Steve Jobs's 2011 death from pancreatic cancer continues to spark debate. He was a food faddist, specifically a consumer only of raw vegan foods, especially fruit, refusing to deviate from that plan even when doctors recommended a diet high in protein and fat to help compensate for his failing pancreas. His office refrigerator was filled with Odwalla juices; he antagonized nonvegan associates by attempting to proselytize among them, as biographer Walter Isaacson has reported:

At a meal with Mitch Kapor, the chairman of Lotus software, Jobs was horrified to see Kapor slathering butter on his bread, and asked, "Have you ever heard of serum cholesterol?" Kapor responded, "I'll make you a deal. You stay away from commenting on my dietary habits, and I will stay away from the subject of your personality."[7]

Defenders of veganism argue that his cancer could be attributed to his occasional forays into protein-eating (a meal of eel sushi has been reported), or perhaps to exposures to toxic metals as a young man tinkering with computers. A case could be made, however, that it was the fruitarian diet that killed him: Metabolically speaking, a diet of fruit is equivalent to a diet of candy, only with fructose instead of glucose, with the effect that the pancreas is strained to constantly produce more insulin. As for the personality issues—the almost manic-depressive mood swings—they could not unreasonably be traced to frequent bouts of hypoglycemia. Incidentally, the sixty-seven-year-old Mitch Kapor is alive and well at the time of this writing.

Similarly, with sufficient ingenuity—or malicious intent—almost any death can be blamed on some failure or mistake of the deceased. Surely Jim Fixx had failed to "listen to his body" when he first felt chest pains and tightness while running, and maybe if Jerry Rubin had been less self-absorbed, he would have looked both ways before crossing the street. Maybe it's just the way the human mind works, but when bad things happen or someone dies, we seek an explanation, and preferably one that features a conscious agency—a deity or spirit, an evildoer or envious acquaintance, even the victim him- or herself. We don't read detective novels to find out that the universe is meaningless, but that, with sufficient information, it all makes sense.

Mass disasters afflicting hundreds or thousands of people of varying degrees of virtue or sinfulness have often required massive supernatural explanations. One of the most confounding disasters in European history was the great earthquake that leveled Lisbon in 1755. The first tremors struck on the morning of All Saints' Day, demolishing many of the city's buildings. After the tremors, a thirty-nine-foot-high tsunami swept up streets full of frantic quake survivors, and this in turn was followed by a huge fire originating in household hearths, which had been left unattended during church services. Altogether, somewhere between thirty thousand and sixty thousand lives were lost, this vast range reflecting the fact that there were no serious efforts to count the dead.

An earlier city-destroying disaster, the 79 CE eruption of Mount Vesuvius, which left the Roman city of Pompeii buried in lava, had occasioned no moralizing, if only because the prevailing deities were not known to be moral exemplars. Jupiter, Juno, and the rest of the pantheon were vain, capricious, and generally indifferent to human suffering. But by the eighteenth century, the pagan gods had all been replaced by a single monotheistic deity who had the double responsibility of being both all-powerful and all-good. This was a tricky combination at best, and the root of the theological puzzle of "theodicy": If God is perfectly good, how can he let bad things happen? True believers rushed in to assert that if he flattened Lisbon, that must be because Lisbon was wicked, which may have been a fair assessment. As one historian observes, in pre-quake Lisbon, the convents usually doubled as brothels[8]—although the moral reckoning is a little complicated by the fact that cathedrals and the local headquarters of the Inquisition toppled or burned along with the dens of iniquity.

Historians can discern a bright side to the Lisbon earthquake: It helped instigate the new intellectual era known as the Enlightenment. While the faithful debated whether it was even worthwhile to try to rebuild the city God had so clearly marked for destruction, when it might be better to devote oneself to prayer and acts of penitence, the French philosopher Voltaire published a lengthy poem refuting the entire idea of a good God:

> *And can you then impute a sinful deed*
> *To babes who on their mothers' bosoms bleed?*
> *Was then more vice in fallen Lisbon found,*
> *Than Paris, where voluptuous joys abound?*
> *Was less debauchery to London known,*
> *Where opulence luxurious holds the throne?*[9]

Voltaire, who dabbled in chemistry and physics in his own home laboratory, proposed that the earthquake was the result of "natural causes," which would eventually be understandable through patient observation. It would not be until the twentieth century that the theory of plate tectonics arose, and with it the notion of an unstable planetary surface composed of shifting puzzle pieces. But Voltaire helped establish that there were no moral lessons to be derived from the carnage of 1755. It was an accident.

But nearly three hundred years after the Lisbon earthquake and the philosophical debates that followed it, we have returned to the habit of dissecting the dead for the moral failings that undid them. Had they neglected important religious rituals and prohibitions, or, in the contemporary version, had they smoked cigarettes and ingested fatty meats? Can we learn anything from their lives and deaths that will help us avoid the same fate?

There is of course a major difference between the intellectual groundwork of the eighteenth century and that of the twenty-first: Our predecessors proceeded from an assumption of human helplessness in the face of a judgmental and all-powerful God who could swoop down and kill tens of thousands at will, while today's assumption is one of almost unlimited *human* power. We can, or think we can, understand the causes of disease in cellular and chemical terms, so we should be able to avoid it by following the rules laid down by medical science: avoiding tobacco, exercising, undergoing routine medical screening, and eating only foods currently considered healthy. Anyone who fails to do so is inviting an early death. Or to put it another way, every death can now be understood as suicide.

Liberal commentators countered that this view represented a kind of "victim-blaming." In her books *Illness as Metaphor* and *AIDS and Its Metaphors*, Susan Sontag argued against the oppressive moralizing of disease, which was increasingly portrayed as an individual problem. The lesson, she said, was "Watch your appetites. Take care of yourself. Don't let yourself go."[10] Even breast cancer, she noted, which has no clear lifestyle correlates, could be blamed on a "cancer personality," sometimes defined in terms of repressed anger, which presumably one could have sought therapy to cure. Little or nothing was said, even by the major breast cancer advocacy groups, about possible environmental carcinogens or carcinogenic medical regimes like hormone replacement therapy. A 1998 official UK "Green Paper" on health summarized that "it is finally up to the individual to choose whether to change their behaviour to a healthier one."[11]

While the affluent struggled dutifully to conform to the latest prescriptions for healthy living—adding whole grains and gym time to their daily plans—the less affluent remained for the most part mired in the old comfortable, unhealthy ways of the past, smoking cigarettes and eating foods they found tasty and affordable. There are some obvious reasons why the poor and the working class resisted the health craze: Gym memberships can be expensive; "health foods" usually cost more than "junk food." But as the classes diverged, the new stereotype of the lower classes as willfully unhealthy quickly fused with their old stereotype as semiliterate louts. I confront this directly in my work as an advocate for a higher minimum wage. Affluent audiences may cluck sympathetically over the miserably low wages offered to blue-collar workers, but they often want to know "why these people don't take better care of themselves," why, for example, do they smoke or eat fast food? Concern for the poor usually comes tinged with criticism.

And contempt. In the 2000s, British celebrity chef Jamie Oliver took it on himself to reform the eating habits of the masses, starting with school lunches. Pizza and burgers were replaced with menu items one might expect to find in a moderately upscale restaurant—fresh greens, for example, and roast chicken. But the experiment was a mortifying failure. Both in the United States and the UK, schoolchildren dumped out their healthy new lunches or stamped them underfoot. Mothers passed burgers to their children through school fences. Administrators complained that the new meals were vastly over budget; nutritionists noted that they were cruelly deficient in calories. In Oliver's defense, it should be observed that ordinary "junk food" is chemically engineered to provide an addictive combination of salt, sugar, and fat. But it probably matters too that he didn't bother to study local eating habits before challenging them, nor did he seem to have given much thought to creatively modifying them. In West Virginia, he alienated parents by bringing a local mother to tears when he publicly announced that the food she normally gave her four children was "killing" them.[12]

There can of course be unfortunate consequences from eating the wrong foods. But what are the "wrong" foods? In the 1980s and '90s, the educated classes turned against fat in all forms, advocating the low-fat diet that, journalist Gary Taubes argues, paved the way for an "epidemic of obesity" as health-seekers switched from cheese cubes to low-fat desserts.[13] The evidence linking dietary fat to poor health had always been shaky, but class prejudice prevailed: Fatty and greasy foods were for the poor and unenlightened; their betters stuck to bone-dry biscotti and fat-free milk. Other nutrients went in and out of style as medical opinion shifted: It turns out that high dietary cholesterol, as in oysters, is not a problem after all, and the doctors have stopped pushing calcium on women over forty. Increasingly, the main villains appear to be sugar and refined carbohydrates, as in hamburger buns. Eat a burger and fries washed down with a large sugary drink, and you will probably be hungry again in a couple of hours, when the sugar rush subsides. If the only cure for that is more of the same, your blood sugar levels may permanently rise, causing the condition we call diabetes.

Special opprobrium is attached to fast food, thought to be the food of the ignorant. Filmmaker Morgan Spurlock spent a month eating nothing but McDonald's offerings to create his famous *Super Size Me*, documenting his twenty-four-pound weight gain and soaring blood cholesterol. I have also spent many weeks eating fast food because it's cheap and filling, but in my case, to no perceptible ill effects. It should be pointed out, though, that I ate selectively, skipping the fries and sugary drinks to double down on the protein. When at a later point a notable food writer called to interview me on the subject of fast food, I started by mentioning my favorites (Wendy's and Popeyes), but it turned out that they were all indistinguishable to him. He wanted a comment on the general category, which was to me like asking what I thought about restaurants.

The Great White Die-Off

If food choices defined the class gap, smoking provided a firewall between the classes. To be a smoker in almost any industrial country is to be a pariah, and most likely a sneak. I grew up in another world, the 1940s and '50s, when cigarettes served not only as a comfort for the lonely but a powerful social glue. People offered each other cigarettes, and lights, indoors as well as outdoors, in bars, restaurants, workplaces, and living rooms, to the point where tobacco smoke became synonymous with human habitation, and, for better or worse, the scent of home. In John Steinbeck's 1936 novel *In Dubious Battle*, a cynical older labor organizer offers a young migrant worker a fresh-rolled cigarette, along with some advice:

> You ought to take up smoking. It's a nice social habit. You'll have to talk to a lot of strangers in your time. I don't know any quicker way to soften a stranger down than to offer him a smoke, or even to ask him for one. And lots of guys feel insulted if they offer you a cigarette and you don't take it. You better start.[14]

My parents smoked; one of my grandfathers could roll a cigarette with one hand; my aunt, who was eventually to die of lung cancer, taught me how to smoke when I was a teenager. And the government seemed to approve. It wasn't till 1975 that the armed forces stopped including cigarettes along with food rations.

As more affluent people gave up the habit, the war on smoking—which was always presented as an entirely benevolent effort—began to look like a war against the working class. When the break rooms offered by employers banned smoking, workers were left to brave the elements outdoors, where you can see them leaning against walls to shelter their cigarettes from the wind. When working-class bars went nonsmoking, their clienteles dispersed to drink and smoke in private, leaving few indoor sites for gatherings and conversations. Escalating cigarette taxes hurt the poor and the working class hardest. The way out is to buy single cigarettes on the streets, but strangely enough the sale of these "loosies" is largely illegal. In 2014 a Staten Island man, Eric Garner, was killed in a chokehold by city police for precisely this crime.[15]

Why do people smoke? The most common explanation, reinforced by Steinbeck, is that peer pressure leads people to start smoking, after which the addictive power of nicotine leaves them without much choice. There has been little exploration of the inherent pleasures of smoking, as if the very mention of them would undercut the antismoking cause. An exception was a 2011 column in which a journalist boldly asserted:

> I *love* smoking, I like the way it tastes after a meal or with a cocktail, I like the way it fends off boredom, I like it on a hot, sweaty summer day and I like it on a cold, crisp winter night....In the end, the ritual and routine of smoking, not to mention the nicotine, puts me at ease and relaxes me.[16]

Nicotine activates the brain's "reward pathways," so that reactivating them becomes a form of self-nurturance and a way of countering pressure and overwork as well as, sometimes, boredom. I once worked in a restaurant in the era when smoking was still permitted in break rooms, and many workers left their cigarettes burning in the common ashtray so that they could catch a puff whenever they had a chance to, without bothering to relight. Everything else they did was for the boss or the customers; smoking was the one thing they did for themselves. In one of the few studies of why people smoke, a British sociologist found that smoking among working-class women was associated with greater responsibilities for the care of family members—again suggesting a kind of defiant self-nurturance.[17]

When the notion of "stress" was crafted in the mid twentieth century, the emphasis was on the health of executives, whose anxieties presumably outweighed those of a manual laborer who had no major decisions to make. It turns out, however, that the amount of stress one experiences—measured by blood levels of the stress hormone cortisol—increases as you move down the socioeconomic scale, with the most stress being inflicted on those who have the least control over their work. In the restaurant industry, stress is concentrated among the people responding to the minute-by-minute demands of customers, not those who sit in corporate offices discussing future menus. Add to these workplace stresses the challenges imposed by poverty and you get a combination that is highly resistant to, for example, antismoking propaganda—as Linda Tirado reported about her life as a low-wage worker with two jobs and two children:

> I smoke. It's expensive. It's also the best option. You see, I am always, always exhausted. It's a stimulant. When I am too tired to walk one more step, I can smoke and go for another hour. When I am enraged and beaten down and incapable of accomplishing one more thing, I can smoke and I feel a little better, just for a minute. It is the only relaxation I am allowed.[18]

Nothing has happened to ease the pressures on low-wage workers. On the contrary, if the old paradigm of a blue-collar job was forty hours a week, an annual two-week vacation, and benefits such as a pension and health insurance, the new expectation is that one will work on demand, as needed, without benefits or guarantees of any kind. Some surveys now find a majority of US retail workers working without regular schedules[19]—on call for when the employer wants them to come and unable to predict how much they will earn from week to week or even day to day. With the rise in "just in time" scheduling, it becomes impossible to plan ahead: Will you have enough money to pay the rent? Who will take care of the children? The consequences of employee "flexibility" can be just as damaging as a program of random electric shocks applied to caged laboratory animals.

Sometime in the first decade of the twenty-first century, demographers began to notice an unexpected uptick in the death rates of poor white Americans. This was not supposed to happen. For almost a century, the comforting American narrative was that better nutrition and medical care would guarantee longer lives for all. It was especially not supposed to happen to whites who, in relation to people of color, have long had the advantage of higher earnings, better access to health care, safer neighborhoods, and of course freedom from the daily insults and harms inflicted on the darker-skinned. But the gap between the life expectancies of blacks and whites has been narrowing. At first, some researchers found the rising mortality rates of poor whites less than surprising: Didn't the poor have worse health habits than the affluent? Didn't they smoke?

According to the *New York Times*, economist Adriana Lleras-Muney, one of the first to note the mortality gap, offered the explanation that "as a group, less educated [and thus on the whole, poorer] people are less able to plan for the future and to delay gratification. If true, that may, for example, explain the differences in smoking rates between more educated people and less educated ones."[20] Another researcher, economist James Smith at the Rand Corporation, amplified on this point a few years later: Poor people don't seem to realize that "a lot of things you might do don't have an immediate negative impact—excessive drinking, smoking, and doing drugs can [feel good in the short term]—but the fact is it's going to kill you in the future."[21]

Poor white Americans were, in other words, killing themselves, and this was not a mere blip in the data. In late 2015, the British economist Angus Deaton won the Nobel Prize for work he had done with fellow economist Anne Case, showing that the mortality gap between wealthy white men and poor ones was widening at a rate of one year each year, and slightly less for women. A couple of months later, "economists at the Brookings Institution found that for men born in 1920, there was a six-year difference in life expectancy between the top 10 percent of earners and the bottom 10 percent. For men born in 1950, that difference more than doubled, to 14 years."[22] Smoking could account for only one-fifth to one-third of the excess deaths. The rest were apparently attributable to alcoholism, opioid addiction, and actual suicide—as opposed to metaphorically killing oneself through unwise lifestyle choices.

But why the excess mortality among poor *white* Americans? In the last few decades, things have not been going well for working-class people of any color. I grew up in an America where a man with a strong back—and better yet, a strong union—could reasonably expect to support a family on his own without a college degree. By 2015, those jobs were long gone, leaving only the kind of work once relegated to women and people of color, in areas like retail, landscaping, and delivery-truck driving. This means that those in the bottom 20 percent of the white income distribution face material circumstances similar to those long familiar to poor blacks, including erratic employment and crowded, hazardous living spaces. When a member of my extended family needed a loan to pay her mortgage, I was surprised to discover that her home was not a house; it was a single-wide trailer she shared with two other family members. Poor whites had always had the comfort of knowing that someone was worse off and more despised than they were; racial subjugation was the ground under their feet, the rock they stood upon, even when their own situation was deteriorating. That slender reassurance is shrinking.

There are some practical reasons too why whites are likely to be more efficient than blacks at killing themselves. For one thing, they are more likely to be gun owners, and white men favor gunshots as a means of suicide. For another, doctors, undoubtedly acting in part on stereotypes of nonwhites as drug addicts, are more likely to prescribe powerful opioid painkillers to whites than to people of color. Pain is endemic among the blue-collar working class, from waitresses to construction workers, and few people make it past fifty without palpable damage to their knees, back, or rotator cuffs. In 2011, the Centers for Disease Control and Prevention declared an "epidemic" of opioid use, in which the victims are mostly white.[23] As opioids became more expensive and closely regulated, users often make the switch to heroin, which varies in strength and can easily lead to accidental overdoses.

It's hard to find historical analogies to the current white-collar die-off in the United States. Perhaps the closest is the sudden drop in male life expectancy associated with the fall of communism in the Soviet Union. As jobs were lost and the old infrastructure of social welfare measures—free medical care and education—came apart in the 1990s, Russian male life expectancy fell from sixty-two to fifty-eight; women's hovered around seventy-four.[24] Other post-communist countries did not suffer such a startling transition, in part because they did not undergo the same "shock therapy" that international financial institutions had prescribed for the Soviet Union. As in America, "lifestyle" factors are easy to invoke: The fall of communism led to an upsurge in alcoholism and alcohol-related deaths.

Or, for a more global and somber analogy, we could reach back to the deadly consequences of European expansionism in the sixteenth through the twentieth centuries, and still ongoing. The number of indigenous people killed in this "single, multi-century, planet-wide exterminatory pulse,"[25] whether by bullets, disease, or mass deportations, has been estimated at fifty million.[26] But when the shooting stopped, the survivors were often left suffering from what could be a fatal malaise, characterized by alcoholism, depression, and suicide. This was the background for anthropologist Claude Lévi-Strauss's 1955 *Tristes Tropiques*: decimated native cultures, stripped of customs, rituals, or traditional means of subsistence, left listless and dispirited by their encounter with the West. The advocacy group Cultural Survival reports that

> throughout the Western Hemisphere, indigenous peoples suffer from high rates of alcoholism and suicide. The same can be said of the peoples of Oceania and northern Russia, as well as the aboriginal groups of Taiwan. Furthermore, we can safely conjecture that dislocation, epidemics, depopulation, and subjugation have put indigenous peoples everywhere at high risk of depression and anxiety.[27]

Like twentieth-century Russian workers or nineteenth-century Polynesians, the American working class—or at least the white part of it—which could once hope for steady work at decent pay, has lost much of its way of life.

In current political conversations, the anomalous mortality of poor white Americans is often elided or confused with the larger problem of economic inequality. Until very recently, any shortcomings the United States experienced in the realm of health and mortality relative to other advanced countries, such as its embarrassingly high rate of infant mortality, could be chalked up to "diversity": The American numbers were being dragged down by the presence of a historically and relentlessly disadvantaged racial minority, or so we were told. But clearly race does not explain everything—poverty itself shortens life spans. What has happened is that the gap between the rich and the poor has widened abruptly in the last forty and even the last five years, to the point where the richest 1 percent of Americans now own 35 percent of the nation's net worth.[28] The trailer parks, tenements, and tent cities of the poor coexist, however uneasily, with the penthouse-topped towers of the rich.

In fact, the gap between rich and poor—not only in the United States but in other highly unequal societies, such as the UK and Israel—has widened to such an extent that a single word, "health," no longer suffices to describe what was once a universally desirable biological status. The increasingly polarized economic situation demands the more nebulous and elastic concept of "wellness." At the lower end of the wealth and income spectrum, wellness presents itself in the form of the corporate wellness programs now offered by about half of employers. These range from in-house gyms to ambitious surveillance programs that subject employees to periodic measurements of quantities like blood pressure and body mass index. Failure to participate or to comply with weight loss goals can mean being forced to pay higher premiums for health insurance or even outright fines, although there is no evidence that such programs either improve employees' health or reduce employers' expenses.[29]

But aside from punitive corporate programs aimed at retail and midlevel white-collar employees, wellness is mainly the domain of the rich, described in the fitness industry as a "luxury pursuit." *Vogue* magazine's online site Style.com goes further, announcing that wellness is "the new luxury status symbol," which can be displayed simply by carrying a yoga tote bag and a bottle of green vegetable-based juice. An advantage of wellness as a status symbol is that it is less likely to incite the envy of the lower classes than, say, furs and diamonds, plus the practice of wellness goes on largely out of sight, in hard-to-access spaces like private gyms and spas. There are hundreds if not thousands of luxury wellness resorts around the world (although some of them may be traditional resorts to which the word "wellness" has been appended for marketing purposes). At their most ambitious, these resorts offer something far more comprehensive than mere "health," which still carries the taint of its old definition as the "absence of disease." Every known modality of self-improvement is on hand: yoga, Rolfing, detoxification, tai chi, and meditation, plus more esoteric practices such as hot stone massages, "sound therapy," often involving Tibetan singing drums, and "phototherapy." At a "destination" wellness resort, the scenery and even the local indigenous people may be enlisted in the healing process:

Our private, customized wellness retreats will reconnect you to your mind, body, and spirit in some of the world's most breathtaking places. We invite you to partake in sacred rituals alongside the Kalahari's Shamans, rebalance your body with private yoga classes in ancient Indian temples, refocus your mind as you chant with monks in Bhutan, and partake in healing practices such as massage, Reiki, and soaking in hot springs at luxurious onsens throughout the Japanese countryside. Whether you find yourself meditating in the foothills of the Himalayas, or engulfed in the peaceful solitude of Botswana's saltpans, our wellness vacations will take you on an adventure of purpose, power, and personal renewal.[30]

No unifying theory—or, of course, cultural source—undergirds the hodgepodge of practices and interventions offered in the name of wellness. But if you read enough of the advertising literature, a common theme emerges, in which the key terms are "harmony," "wholeness," and "balance." To the extent that there is a philosophy here, it is holism, the source of the familiar adjective, "holistic." Everything—mind, body, and spirit, diet and attitude—is connected and must be brought into alignment for maximum effectiveness, whether to achieve "power" and "personal renewal" or just to lose a few pounds. Conflict may be endemic to the human world, with all its jagged inequalities, but it must be abolished within the individual. To what end? To feel good, of course, which is the same as feeling powerful. Put in more mechanical terms, wellness is the means to remake oneself into an ever more perfect self-correcting machine capable of setting goals and moving toward them with smooth determination. As Søren Kierkegaard wrote in a famous devotional text, "purity of heart is to will one thing,"[31] although he did not mean that one thing was stronger quadriceps.

CHAPTER SEVEN

The War Between
Conflict and Harmony

I f the body—or the "mindbody" or whatever we are individually comprised of—somehow "wants" to act as a
unified whole, then it should be easy enough to bring it under our conscious control. All we have to do is use the mind
to encourage this natural urge toward wholeness, and inevitably, with the help of meditation, yoga poses, and a
mindfully abstemious diet, wellness will follow. It was that
simple.

The concepts of wellness and wholeness first wafted into
American culture in the 1970s along with the scent of
patchouli—hence the later derogation of some nonstandard practices as "hippie bullshit." In matters related to
health, the old paradigm had been scientific reductionism:
To understand something, you first have to take it apart
and, using techniques like dissection, microscopy, and the
fractionation of tissue into subcellular fragments, study its
constituent parts. But in the new paradigm, promoted by
the counterculture of the 1960s but also traceable to Emer-
son and any number of Eastern and European mystics, the

focus was on the interconnections between the parts, and hence on the whole, which was increasingly assumed to be "more than the sum of its parts." In some versions, the entire cosmos was depicted as a single entity containing each one of us, or at least our souls or spirits—a perspective that seems more consistent with Eastern mysticism and the emerging psychedelic drug culture than dreary old math-ridden, reductionist science. According to counterculture chronicler Theodore Roszak, the hippies and flower children aimed for nothing less than "the subversion of the scientific world view itself."[1]

We may think of the counterculture as a laid-back philosophical stance opposed to the very concept of control, but holism opened a new avenue of control—exercised by the mind over the body. Mind and body were disconnected in the reductionist scheme of things; it was not even clear that they belonged in the same sentence. From a holistic viewpoint, though, they were continuous, forming almost a single substance, the "mindbody," which could be accessed through conscious effort. How exactly the mind-body connection works can be comically difficult to explain, as in a passage from a book called *Integrative Holistic Health, Healing, and Transformation*:

> When the mind is filled with negative imaginings, anxiety and depression producing neuropeptides are created. Additionally, the limbic system [of the brain] gets caught in a continuous negative feedback loop resulting in the amygdala affecting the sympathetic response from the autonomic nervous system affecting bodily changes reminding

the individual of past trauma thus producing more anxiety and imaginings which affect the amygdala, etc.[2]

If you didn't understand that, don't worry. Aside from the syntactical disarray illustrated by this quote, it should be pointed out that there is no solid evidence that, aside from the effects of extreme stress, negative thoughts affect physical health, or that optimists live longer than pessimists.* Nevertheless, the author reassures us that "participating in a holistic health program or going to a practitioner often brings back a sense of control and hope, which, in and of itself can strengthen the body's capacity to fight disease and stay healthy."[3] An amulet would probably work just as well.

No new discoveries or scientific insights accompanied the new holistic paradigm. It was not based on a theory but on a sensibility that, by the late twentieth century, was gaining a measure of legitimacy from something that could not have been more temperamentally different from the counterculture. This was "systems analysis," a fad that first took hold in the world of corporate management. I would never have encountered it if I hadn't spent a few months working as a "program policy analyst" at the New York City budget bureau. What that title meant exactly was never explained to me, nor was "systems analysis," which was being installed in the city government by the Rand Corporation and seemed to involve making decisions based on

---

* See my book *Bright-Sided: How the Relentless Promotion of Positive Thinking Has Undermined America.*

quantitative data and doing it as "systematically" as possible. (Although at any moment some new political priority could arise from the mayor's office to override the planners' logical and numerically sound recommendations.) The key insight was that human organizations, such as armies, governments, and corporations, are "systems" or "complex systems," like the human body itself, in which all the parts need to be considered together.

Oddly enough, given the assumed countercultural lineage of all things holistic, the chief promoter of systems analysis was a man surely innocent of psychedelic or mystical experience—Robert McNamara, the secretary of defense under Presidents Kennedy and Johnson. When he was plucked from the Ford Motor Company for the defense job, McNamara was initially shocked by the *un*systemlike nature of the Pentagon, where the different services—army, navy, and so forth—competed for resources with little or no centralized control. His solution had been to introduce a "program policy budget system," the template for the one I later encountered in the New York City Budget Bureau. In the military, as in the budget bureau, it seems to have been largely interpreted as an emphasis on quantitative goals and metrics—most famously, "body counts." So, piling one irony on top of another, the effort to rationalize military planning found itself enlisted into the service of America's fundamentally irrational war in Vietnam, and that effort was vaguely in synch with countercultural yearning for wholeness.

Perhaps the most spectacular, and most spectacularly wrong, application of systems analysis was the Gaia hypothesis, advanced by chemist and atmospheric scientist James Lovelock in 1974. Influenced by the increasingly popular science of ecology and made intuitively plausible by the first photos of our planet from space, the hypothesis proposed that Earth and all that live on it comprise a single "system," in fact, a self-regulating, living system in which the parts (humans, for example, or algae) interact to make Earth habitable for living creatures. That majestic image of a blue planet in space came to symbolize all that was good and desirable—wholeness, unity, ecology, interconnectedness, peace, harmony. It also decorated the cover of the *Whole Earth Catalog*, which featured subsistence farming techniques, outdoor gear, and DIY technologies for hippies and geeks seeking self-sufficiency. Humans were subunits of that greater whole represented by the planet Earth, although unfortunately the smooth-running system that was Gaia has never figured out how to correct for the profligate human consumption of fossil fuels.

If systems analysis could not provide scientific backup for the new paradigm of wholeness, it at least helped reinforce its cultural legitimacy. As Encyclopedia.com tells us, in three sentences that are notable for containing the words "system" or "systems" nine times, the idea of systems was everywhere, and seemed to embrace wholeness in any form:

During the second half of the twentieth century amalgams of the terms *system* and *systems* became ubiquitous. Computer and operating systems were joined by biological, business, and political systems. Systems science and systems engineering were complemented by systems management, systems medicine, and the practice of looking at the earth as a system.[4]

At times the notion of a "system" and a "whole" were almost indistinguishable. For example, something called the "mindful economics movement" sought "to engage a holistic and systems analysis of economic problems associated with capitalism."[5] "Holistic" was good; anything less was a capitulation to the Enlightenment, science, capitalism, or whatever other evil force was believed to have smashed the human world into antagonistic fragments. To be holistic was to be kind, peaceable, and inclusive, which of course is how every vendor of services seeks to be seen. You can even find "holistic dentists," although a focus on any particular part of the body seems like a violation of holism.

It can be hard to discern any possible common ground between the two paradigms. At the extreme of scientific reductionism we have the fabled doctor who is so lost in the "parts" that he or she can no longer see the whole human, and refers to a patient as "the gall bladder in room 302." As we have seen in earlier chapters, medical education—beginning with the first corpse dissection—seems intent on removing any emotional connection between the patient and the physician. The patient is objectified, her conscious participation being required only in the form of "compliance." At the other extreme of congeniality would be the massage therapist I went to for lymphedema following surgery. She was a chatty, empathetic young woman, who in a dimly lit room gently fingered my chest and arms to the accompaniment of recorded trance music. (Not surprisingly, several sessions of this did nothing for the incipient swelling, which I insisted on measuring before and after.) To its critics, the scientific approach is cold, rationalist even, in the view of feminist theorist Vandana Shiva, "imperialistic," while alternative approaches are soothing, nurturing, and somehow aligned with the cosmos. The philosophical gap here is at least as great as the one thought to exist between science and religion—and wars have been fought over less.

Spats still break out from time to time, as in 2005 when the Society for Neuroscience provoked protests by inviting the Dalai Lama to speak on meditation and mindfulness at its annual conference. But even by the late twentieth century a fertile area of overlap had opened up between science, particularly quantum physics, and what we might loosely call the counterculture. Timothy Leary, the LSD pioneer, and Werner Erhard, the founder of EST, were both attracted to quantum physics, which a layperson could readily sample at venues such as Big Sur and the Santa Fe Institute. Meanwhile, some scientists and historians of science were beginning to mutter about the need for a more holistic approach within science itself. Philosopher of science Evelyn Fox critiqued reductionist biology's emphasis on "master molecules," such as DNA, at the expense of the whole organism. At a somewhat less respectable academic level, the physicist Fritjof Capra discerned a continuity between quantum mechanics and Eastern mysticism and asserted that the natural world was not made up of discrete subunits, but of interacting vibrations. The path was clear for the explosive growth of integrative medicine in the twenty-first century, in which the philosophical contradictions between the different treatment modalities could be dismissed with a wave of a hand and a mumbled reference to quantum physics.

Holistic Biology

By the late twentieth century, there is no question that medical science needed some sort of paradigm shift, if only to accommodate the fact that a "whole person"—body in addition to mind—is not well represented by a cadaver. Not only do we think and feel, but we react to the world in microscopic ways that are not visible to our minds and not easily accessible to our willpower or control. We bleed when cut, and if we are lucky the blood clots without our conscious intervention. The "system" that is a whole person contains many levels and parts. Some are macroscopic and some are microscopic; some are material, such as an organ, others apparently immaterial, as in the case of thoughts. How they interact to create a stable, or at least briefly stable, system has been the ongoing challenge to biological science.

The assumption, which has been around long enough to be almost unquestioned, has been that all parts and layers of the body work in concert. When we talk about human biology we are of course talking about the biology of multicellular beings composed of subunits like tissues and cells. All these tissues and cells are presumed to work in harmony, each selflessly performing its assigned function, like obedient citizens of a benign dictatorship. Heart cells beat in unison, liver cells store glucose, red blood cells carry oxygen. Anything else would be a disaster, right? Thus the biology of multicellular beings is biased toward a holistic outlook. We aren't content to describe, say, a kidney; we want to know what its *function* is—what it does in service to the whole.

The assignment of functions to different parts or sub-units of the body goes back at least to the seventeenth century, when the English physician William Harvey figured out that the beating of the heart keeps the blood circulating, although why circulation was important was still not clear at the time. Prior to this discovery, anatomists had been content to describe and locate the organs, leaving it to physiologists or metaphysicians to explain what the organs actually did and how they fit into the body as a whole. According to Harvey, the heart had a "function," and, as biologists quickly inferred, so must all other subunits and parts of the body. Pick up a contemporary biology textbook and you will find it thickly populated by the word "function," sometimes applied even to molecules. A 2014 cell biology textbook finds various ways of describing the commitment of cells and tissues to their functions: They have the "responsibility" or "task" of performing these functions, or they are said to be "specialized" to perform them,[6] much like soldiers in an army or professors in a university.

Harvey's discovery revealed the body to be a kind of machine, cleverly built up out of interconnecting, smoothly cooperating parts that had no volition of their own. As a seventeenth-century Italian anatomist proclaimed, "A human body, as to its natural actions…is truly nothing else but a complex of chymico-mechanical motions, depending on such principles as are purely mathematical."[7] This mechanical view, which still dominates biology today, in no way challenged religion: After all, an extraordinarily brilliant designer must be behind the whole thing, or must at least have breathed life into some inert prior substance. And indeed the more we learn about how the body works, the more supernaturally marvelous its working seems. Consider how the body heals its wounds. First, a cascade of chemical reactions closes the lesion by making blood clot. At the same time, cells rush in from the bone marrow and other sites to chase out microbes, remove damaged tissue, and replace it with fresh, intact cells and tissues, so that we are prepared for any future wounds.

If the body is a perfect clockwork mechanism, this was, according to a cheap and dirty form of Darwinism, because perfection was inevitable. Bodily parts that didn't work, or work optimally, would be eliminated by natural selection, leaving only the "fittest" organisms to survive and breed. In the sociobiology that thrived in the 1960s, there was an evolutionary rationale for everything, and any trait or physical characteristic that did not contribute to the survival of the species would be weeded out as a waste of energy. This led to a noxious defense of the status quo, often denounced by feminists as "determinism": We are the way we are—say, warlike or male supremacist—because to be any other way would be less "fit," and the sculptor that shaped us this way is not God but natural selection.

The trouble was that many things cannot be explained in terms of "fitness," including vestigial characteristics like male nipples and the appendix, as well as purely structural features that just seem to be required by the available "designs" in our genomes. Biologists Stephen Jay Gould and Richard Lewontin deemed that such structural features are the analog of "spandrels" in the design of cathedrals: They don't "do" anything except to fill in a preexisting pattern of arches. Natural selection, Gould and Lewontin pointed out, is not the only force governing evolution, nor had Darwin ever suggested that it was. Changes in the environment—climate changes or the sudden arrival of an asteroid—can cause the extinction of whole species that may have been supremely well adapted the moment before disaster struck. Meanwhile, apparently useless features like male nipples may be conserved over generations simply because the plan for them remains in our genetic material.

So the unacknowledged bias in biology is optimistic, even utopian. Our bodies are perfectly adapted to the environment—or at least to the environment our distant ancestors faced—and they are that way because they could be no other way. In their critique of evolutionary biology, Gould and Lewontin invoked Voltaire's insanely optimistic Professor Pangloss, who had declared that everything was for the best in this "best of all possible worlds." The same could be said of the "functional" view of the body, which carries with it the assumption that all the parts and subunits act in harmony, ever alert to the needs of the whole. This is how we are introduced to biology as students—as the study of ideally functioning complex systems in which disease and death are disappointing aberrations.

But all is not well in this best of all possible worlds,

and the aberrations are too common, not to mention too dramatic, to dismiss. Consider cancer, which is one of the leading causes of death worldwide. Many cancers can be blamed on chemical agents or radiation from outside the body, such as cigarette smoke or occupational hazards like benzene, but so far only about 60 percent of cancers can be traced to particular carcinogens.[8] For example, no carcinogens have been discovered to explain cancers of the breast, colon, or prostate. All we know is that individual cells within these organs sometimes break ranks and start reproducing madly, creating tumors that can destroy the entire organism. Or consider autoimmune diseases, such as rheumatoid arthritis and multiple sclerosis, which afflict 5 to 8 percent of the population and arise when the immune system abandons its designated "function," which is to protect the body, and attacks the body itself.[9] The body's own immune cells have also been implicated in the development of coronary artery disease, the greatest single cause of mortality in the United States and Europe.

The functionalist view of the body is still immensely helpful, but only if we remember that it is an *approximation*. Most skin cells, for example, behave as we would expect them to if their functions are to serve as a protection against the outside world, to perspire, and to provide us with tactile experience. But some will become cancerous and attempt to take over the entire body—and what is the "function" of melanoma? We need to admit that instead of acting as a harmonious whole, the body can serve as a battleground where its own cells and tissues meet in mortal combat.

The potential theoretical basis for intrabody conflict had been laid out by Rudolf Virchow in the late nineteenth century, when he proposed that the smallest living subunit of the body was the cell, and that all cells arose from other cells. It was the latter proposition, expressed as *Omnis cellula e cellula*, that tended to attract the most attention because it implied that even the most ferocious cancer cell was the descendant of a peaceable, law-abiding healthy cell. But in some ways it was the first proposition—that the cell was the smallest living subunit of the body—that perhaps should have generated more excitement. At the time of Virchow's work, other biologists were beginning to succeed in cultivating body cells *outside* of the body—in what came to be called "tissue cultures," bathed in a nutrient fluid such as a serum. The stage was set, by the beginning of the twentieth century, for a thorough study of these curious microscopic entities—cells—that make up living organisms.

But this was the road not taken. The middle of the twentieth century brought the stunning discovery of the structure of DNA and its role in heredity. Almost overnight, biology entered its extreme reductionist phase, zipping right past cells to get to the more glamorous molecular level, where DNA, RNA, and proteins ruled. Cancer research came to focus on the DNA mutations that predispose cells to a career of selfish reproduction. Immunology downplayed the cellular dynamics of the immune system in favor of an obsession with antibodies—the protein molecules that can mark a "foreign" cell, like a microbe, for destruction—although it is chiefly specialized immune cells called macrophages that do the destroying. My first thesis adviser at Rockefeller University won a Nobel Prize for elucidating the structure of antibody molecules. My second thesis adviser got far less recognition, and a much smaller lab, for his work on how macrophages kill and digest their prey.

Cancer is hard enough to explain: Why would a cell undertake a campaign of conquest that can only end in that cell's own death? But cancer is commonly traced to errors in cell division, and it is easy to imagine such errors leading a healthy cell to produce two cancerous daughter cells. Autoimmune diseases, like rheumatoid arthritis and multiple sclerosis, in which the immune system attacks healthy tissue within the body, pose a more vexing philosophical problem for biology. It is possible to imagine a single cell producing cancerous offspring, but it is not so easy to see how the many delicate mechanisms making up the immune response—which involve interactions between multiple types of cells—could be mobilized against the body's own tissues. Posed with the possibility of such an attack, biologist Paul Ehrlich simply postulated the existence of a built-in *horror autotoxicus*, or "horror of self-poisoning," that would somehow prevent such hideous mistakes. How could there not be such a thing, since "life cannot harm itself," as the "dogma" of *horror autotoxicus* put it? For an organism to undermine itself would be, in Ehrlich's words, "dysteleological in the highest degree,"[10] meaning that it would serve no purpose.

Fifty years later, in the middle of the twentieth century, the Australian immunologist Frank Macfarlane Burnet took Ehrlich's dictum about the impossibility of autoimmune disorders a little further when he proclaimed that the true function of the immune system was a metaphysical one: to distinguish "self" and "non-self"—the latter being foreign material such as microbes and the former being one's own tissues. These are terms drawn from psychology or philosophy; they are "nebulous," as philosopher of science Alfred I. Tauber has pointed out, adding that "the self can hardly be viewed as a scientific concept."[11] In fact, it was barely even a concept at all until about the seventeenth century, when languages such as English and German began to use the word "self" as something other than an intensifier (as in "I did it myself"). Then, as we shall see in a later chapter, the "self" began to replace the "soul" as a special kind of kernel within each individual, walled off in part from everyone else. Attention turned inward, as people were encouraged to know them*selves* through, for example, the widespread use of mirrors, the writing of journals and autobiographies, and the painting of portraits, often self-portraits. "Western individualism" was born, along, eventually, with psychoanalysis and any number of afflictions of the self.

So why did Burnet choose such a "nebulous" and patently unscientific concept to explain the work of the immune system? Some scholars have speculated that he was influenced, like so many people of his class, by Freud, and perhaps actually attracted by the aura of subjectivity that hovers around the notion of the self. He could, after all, have used some other term like "the organism" or "the individual" to describe what the immune system is trying to maintain. But if he was looking for a way to talk about the organism versus the "others," generally meaning foreign invaders like microbes, the self/non-self distinction was apt enough. At the heart of immunology is a military metaphor: Non-self is the enemy, usually represented by a bacterium or a virus, and has to be destroyed by the immune system, while "self," meaning the body's own tissues, of course has to be left alone. For example, a popular 1987 book, optimistically entitled *The Body Victorious*, described the immune system as

> reminiscent of military defence, with regard to both weapon technology and strategy. Our internal army has at its disposal swift, highly mobile regiments, shock troops, snipers, and tanks. We have soldier cells which, on contact with the enemy, at once start producing homing missiles whose accuracy is overwhelming...[as well as] reconnaissance squads, an intelligence service and a defence staff which determines the location and strength of troops to be deployed.[12]

The military metaphor can even be tapped to help explain—or excuse—autoimmune diseases. Any human society within a spear's throw of potential enemies needs some kind of defensive force—minimally, an armed group who can defend against invaders. But there are risks to maintaining a garrison or, beyond that, a standing army: The warriors may get greedy and turn against their own people, demanding ever more food and other resources. Similarly, in the case of the body, without immune cells we would be helpless in the face of invading microbes. With them, we face the possibility of treasonous attacks on our "selves"—the autoimmune diseases that Burnet at one point likened to "a mutiny in the security forces of a country."[13]

In fact, no compelling evolutionary explanation for the existence of autoimmune disease has been offered—just the excuse that the immune cells, despite their supposed function of distinguishing self from non-self, sometimes make a "mistake." And why should that be? One popular hypothesis, proposed in 1989, is that the relatively hygienic environments of affluent societies do not give immune cells enough practice in facing their "real" enemies from the microbial world. They grow up, in other words, soft and pampered. But today there is increasing acknowledgment that the link between lack of childhood exposure is not one of cause and effect. One possibility is that highly hygienic environments may simply allow more children to live long enough to develop an autoimmune disease.[14] As Burnet commented, "one cannot discuss autoimmune disease without getting into deep water philosophically."[15]

We could say, in retrospect, that Burnet was torn between two paradigms: One, the holistic, utopian one, saw the body or organism as a well-ordered mechanism, evolutionarily ordained to be exactly as it is. In the other emerging paradigm, which could be called *dystopian*, the organism is a site of constant conflict—as between cancer cells and normal cells or between the immune system and the other tissues in the body. The conflict may result in some sort of compromise in which, for example, the disease settles into a chronic condition. Or it may end, sooner rather than later, in the death of the organism. These two paradigms, utopian and dystopian, may coexist in the same individual mind, Burnet's for example, but to my knowledge they have yet to square off in open combat. There however was a near collision in the early 1990s, for anyone who was paying attention, and it was not about autoimmune disease or cancer, but about something more normal and apparently healthy—menstruation.

Blood Feuds

The onset of menstruation can be appalling, even terrifying, to the young girl who experiences it. There may be painful cramps, leaky tampons or pads, bouts of anemia. Yet, at least among the affluent and educated, every effort is made to normalize this oddly violent occurrence, even to prettify it. A parenting website advises:

> It's also important for parents to paint the process of menstruation in a positive light. If a mother refers to her period as "the curse," her daughter might get a negative impression of the whole experience. Instead, mothers can explain that monthly periods are a natural and wonderful part of being a woman. After all, without them, women couldn't become mothers.[16]

Undeterred by the question of why a twelve-year-old girl should find it "wonderful" that she is now capable of becoming pregnant, the positive pro-menstrual propaganda goes on in its upbeat way. A writer for the American Psychological Association offers "another way to keep-it-positive":

> Some parents have successfully put together a Welcome to Womanhood Basket that might include chocolate, a heating pad, hygiene supplies and perhaps a good book on the topic (or a novel from her favorite author), if she doesn't already have one.[17]

Somehow, the gift of a heating pad and hygiene supplies may seem more ominous than welcoming.

In the "positive" view, menstruation has a serious biological function. Every month, at least in humans, the lining of the uterus grows thick, supposedly to provide a soft cushion for any fertilized eggs that find their way into it. If no embryo implants, the uterus sheds this lining, if only because it would be costly, in a caloric sense, to maintain it—hence the mess of blood and tissue fragments that make up the menstrual discharge. But repeated monthly over decades, the shedding of the uterine lining is itself very costly; women typically lose a pint of blood a year and sometimes several more, creating the risk of anemia. So, if natural selection prevails, and if it works to optimize a species' fitness, why do we menstruate so copiously? In particular, why do humans lose so much more blood than any other creature?

The answer—or at least *an* answer—came from an unlikely source. In 1993, Margie Profet, a thirty-five-year-old with no academic background in biology, proposed that the real function of menstruation is to cleanse the vagina of pathogens that may have been introduced by an intruding penis.[18] I welcomed her hypothesis, which seemingly made the case that menstruation is not a result of female "uncleanness," as patriarchal religions had insisted. Catholic churches, for example, had barred menstruating women; Jewish law required women to undergo a ritual bath after their periods. But according to Profet's theory, menstruation, for all its messiness, was actually an effort to maintain the naturally pristine condition of the female body—a sort of douche in reverse. Within a couple of years, Profet had won a MacArthur "genius award" and been profiled in *Scientific American*, *Omni*, *Time*, and *People*. She became the exemplar of the kind of optimistic biology in which everything "happens for a reason," that reason being to preserve the individual organism and propagate the species. There was still conflict in her model, but only the ancient conflict between humans (or other mammals) and their traditional enemy, microbes.

I tracked her down in the late 1990s to ask a question based on my years of study into the effect of animal predators on human evolution and history, plus my own experience of warnings you are likely to encounter in bear-ridden wild areas: Might not copious menstruation have been a risk factor for predator attacks, especially in the carnivore-ridden "evolutionary environment"? Her terse answer— that "humans are not a cryptic species"—was biologically uninformed, since a "cryptic species" is not one that has to hide from predators, but one that is morphologically identical to a species with a different genome. But mine was only one of a growing number of questions about her theory. Other critics brought up the lack of data on the cleansing effect of the menstrual flow and her failure to explain the fact that human menstruation is so much more copious than that of any other mammal. In fact, very few mammals menstruate at all, and the few that do—other "higher" primates, some bats, and the elephant shrew—lose far less blood than humans, although there is no evidence that the semen of their males is any less germ-ridden than that of human males. Profet's other much-heralded theoretical proposal—that the "morning sickness" characteristic of human pregnancy served to protect the fetus from exposure to foods that might cause birth defects—was similarly assailed, and in about 2004, Margie Profet simply disappeared, only to resurface in 2012 and rejoin her family of origin after a period of poverty and illness.[19]

Today the emerging scientific consensus about menstruation hinges on conflict *within* our species—a possibility that would until recently have been deeply disturbing to biologists. In this view, the buildup of the uterine lining does not serve to entice embryos to implant, but to *prevent* all but the most robust and agile embryos from ever having a chance. I will not attempt to trace the lineage of this counterintuitive idea, except to say that another renegade scientist, Robert Trivers of Rutgers, had argued in the 1970s that the father and mother have different genetic interests at stake. Put crudely, the father "wants"—or more accurately, his genes should want—the embryos he has fertilized to implant and live; the mother's interest is in destroying any potentially defective embryos that might waste her energy on a fruitless pregnancy. Trivers, who is no less a fascinating character than Profet, deserves a book of his own, and in fact has written one, *Wild Life*, that has less to say about science than about his adventurous career, including his membership in the Black Panther Party and long residency in Jamaica. Maybe these experiences gave him the moxie to challenge the more harmonious and utopian tendencies in biology. Not only did he find deadly competition between the sexes even in their most intimate moments, but he proposed that our genomes contain many stretches of DNA (often subsumed under the label "junk DNA") that are truly "selfish" in the sense that they

> have discovered ways to spread and persist without contributing to organismal fitness. At times, this means encoding actions that are diametrically opposed to those of the majority of genes. As a consequence, most organisms are not completely harmonious wholes and the individual is, in fact, divisible.[20]

Trivers's work seems to have emboldened his friend, Harvard biologist David Haig, to offer a far more dystopian view of reproduction than anything Profet and her admirers could have imagined. In 1993, the same year that Profet published her work on menstruation, Haig put forth the surprising view that pregnancy was shaped by "maternal-fetal competition." The fetus and the placenta that attaches it to the maternal bloodstream strive to extract more nutrients from the mother, while maternal tissue fights to hold on to its nutrients—often to the detriment of the mother. For example, the fetus may interfere with maternal insulin production, leading to elevated blood sugar levels that are injurious to the mother but deliciously nourishing to the fetus. Or the fetus and placenta may release chemicals that raise the mother's blood pressure—apparently to guarantee a ready flow of nutrients to the fetus—although at some risk to the mother and ultimately to the fetus as well.

But the maternal/fetal battle begins before implantation, when the embryo and its placenta have to fight their way through endometrial lining to get access to the maternal bloodstream. As evolutionary biologist Suzanne Sadedin, who once studied with Haig, wrote:

> Far from offering a nurturing embrace, the endometrium is a lethal testing-ground which only the toughest embryos survive. The longer the female can delay that placenta reaching her bloodstream, the longer she has to decide if she wants to dispose of this embryo without significant cost. The embryo, in contrast, wants to implant its placenta as quickly as possible, both to obtain access to its mother's rich blood, and to increase her stake in its survival. For this reason, the endometrium got thicker and tougher—and the fetal placenta got correspondingly more aggressive.[21]

In other words, a kind of arms race has gone on between the human endometrium and the human embryo/placental combination. Human placentas are extraordinarily tough fighters compared to those of other species, and our endometria are correspondingly thick and forbidding. Hence the uniquely heavy flow that human females experience—the cramps, bloodstained panties, and perhaps also the widespread cultural notion that women are peculiarly disabled versions of men.

Many phases of women's reproductive cycle, from menstruation to labor, resemble the kind of inflammatory response the human body usually mounts when invaded by pathogens, except that in the reproductive case the targets are not pathogens but human cells and tissues. Menstruation, for example, is not the gentle, autumnal-sounding process of "shedding" an endometrial lining that it is usually described as. When no embryo implants, the uterus releases chemical signals summoning immune cells to come in from the bloodstream and devour its thick endometrial lining, which quickly becomes a killing field, with the debris pouring out of the vagina. Fortunately, during most of human existence, thanks to frequent pregnancies and lengthy periods of lactation, human females probably endured very few menstrual periods during their lifetimes.

So far no adequate explanation has been found for the fact that among humans, about 80 percent of those who suffer from autoimmune diseases are female, suggesting that as holistic "systems," men are much better designed than women. Or it may be that we should see autoimmune diseases as just another part of the greater reproductive burden borne by women: All the inflammatory storms whipped up by menstruation and pregnancy may lead to a hazardous level of immune sensitivity, or, to put it in Burnet's vague philosophical terms, maybe pregnancy and the preparations for it inherently blur the distinction between self and non-self.

But the point is that intrabody conflict—between cells

and their own sibling cells within the same organism—is not confined to pathological conditions like cancer and autoimmune diseases, where it can be traced to a mutation or described as a "mistake." Deadly combat among cells is part of how the body, and especially the human body, conducts its normal business, which certainly includes reproduction. If cells are alive and can seemingly act in their own interests against other parts of the body or even against the entire organism, then we may need to see ourselves less as smoothly running "wholes" that can be controlled by conscious human intervention, and more as confederations, or at least temporary alliances, of microscopic creatures.

It is disconcerting to think of the biological self, or body, as a collection of tiny selves. The image that comes to mind is the grotesque portrait of a super-sized king in the frontispiece of philosopher Thomas Hobbes's *Leviathan*: On close inspection, the king turns out to be composed of hundreds of little people crowded into his arms and torso. Hobbes's point was that human societies need autocratic leaders; otherwise they risk degenerating into a "war of all against all." But no "king" rules the community of cells that makes up the body. Despite, or sometimes because of, all the communications—chemical and electrical—that connect the cells of the body, disagreements and mixed signals can always occur. What we need is a paradigm that includes not only the marvelous harmony within living organisms, but the conflicts that routinely break out.

CHAPTER EIGHT

Cellular Treason

What are these potentially fractious subunits—or "building blocks," as they are sometimes called—of the body, and how can we effectively control them? One of the first cells a biology student is likely to encounter through a microscope is not a subunit of anything. It is a free-living creature in its own right—a single-celled organism called an amoeba. Amoebae, which are easily found in pond water, swim through their environment searching for edible morsels, which they can then engulf with a pseudopod and ingest. I came across them in the laboratory of Maria Rudzinska, with whom I endured a few-weeks-long tutorial along my winding path to a PhD. Her lab was the size of a closet and she seemed annoyed at my presence, a situation that was not improved by my failure to see the relevance of her pet cells to my long-term interest in advancing human health. I was not interested in cells at all, those tiny lipid sacs containing proteins and nucleic acids. They were, from my thoroughly reductionist point of view, just distractions on the way to the real action, which took place at the chemical level that could only be accessed by bursting the cell membrane and grinding its contents into sludge. It even occurred to me that I had not been assigned to Rudzinska because she had anything to teach me, but simply because we shared the anomaly of being female in an overwhelmingly male research institute. Certainly her amoebae were not the evolutionary progenitors of, or even models for, anything human.

It took a couple of years before I began to appreciate events at the cellular level, and decades more, in fact, before I could see the connection between the lives of amoebae and those of the cells in our own bodies. One of the things that held me back was that amoebae are autonomous creatures, while the cells in our bodies obviously are not: They have "functions" to perform. But suppose that body cells, or some of them anyway, some of the time, are even a little bit autonomous?

To the extent that the individual subunits of the body, the cells, are capable of acting on their own, there is always the possibility of mayhem. One can imagine fetal cells escaping from the fetus to pop up years later in some remote part of the mother's tissue, or an entire pregnancy being derailed when an embryo decides to implant somewhere other than in the uterus—in a fallopian tube or even the abdominal cavity. Or cancer cells from other parts of the body could occasionally sneak past the blood/brain barrier to become a fifth column among the neurons that do our thinking for us.

In fact, each of these things occurs: Women who have borne children often contain cells from the fetuses they have carried, making these women *chimera*, or mixtures of different individuals. Furthermore, in 1 or 2 percent of all pregnancies, the embryo arbitrarily attaches itself somewhere other than the uterus, resulting in a life-threatening situation for the mother. Even stranger, breast cancer cells have been caught "disguising" themselves as neurons to colonize the brain. Nor should we be surprised by these outbreaks of self-assertion on the part of cells and small groups of cells. Autoimmune diseases involve an apparently spontaneous attack by immune cells on other body cells; cancer is a mad pursuit of lebensraum originating in a single cell or a small group of cells.

Fortunately, from the point of view of the organism as a whole, there are plenty of mechanisms to keep adventurous cells in place. Tissue cells are bound to each other by "intercellular glue" as well as by "junctions," some of them so tight as to be almost unbreakable. As an additional precaution, organs are often enclosed in membranes that may be difficult or impossible for a cell to breach. Then there is the steady hail of chemical signals that one cell receives from others, some of them sent from considerable distances. We can translate very few of these signals, and they appear to say things like "Danger!" or "Come here right away!" And—who knows?—some of the messages may be propagandistic, urging cells to carry on stalwartly with their appointed tasks. Then there is the final sanction for a recalcitrant cell: death. Signals come in saying "Die!" and, in a process called apoptosis, the cell obligingly shuts down its metabolism, folds neatly into its membrane, and awaits disposal.

But there are some cells that are required, by their agreed-upon "function" in the body, to *be* adventurous, inquisitive, and even aggressive: leucocytes, for the most part, or the white blood cells that fight microbial diseases. Like red blood cells, many leucocytes originate in the bone marrow and are carried around passively by the bloodstream. Others, however, are capable of moving on their own, even through the dense and slippery spaces between cells in a tissue. With the exception of stem cells, there is probably no cell in the body more versatile than the macrophage, which originates, like so many other leucocytes, in the bone marrow. Immature macrophages, called monocytes, are released into the bloodstream, where they may become attracted to a stationary object, like a dead or injured cell, and settle down to devour it. As the macrophage eats, it grows and becomes "activated"—filled with vacuoles containing digestive enzymes that allow it to eat still more. My PhD research eventually involved "harvesting" macrophages from mice and studying this transformation. Although its significance was unclear to me, I could see immediately that a mature macrophage resembles nothing so much as a free-living amoeba. The resemblance is so striking that it has tempted some scientists to speculate that there may be some kind of evolutionary connection between the two types of cells, although of course they come from totally unrelated lineages.[1] Like a free-living amoeba, a macrophage can move around by extending a pseudopod and dragging itself along; it can dispose of dead or injured cells in a wound; it can attack and eat microbes that have found their way into the body.

As the all-purpose handyman of the body, the macrophage has gotten very little respect from mainstream science. It's a blue-collar worker, and since it's responsible for removing cell corpses and other trash, it's been called the "garbage collector" of the body and even, given its lethal capacities, a "thug." The macrophage's M.O. as a killer is indeed rather brutal and thuglike: It engulfs its prey in its cell membrane and proceeds to digest it through the same process of phagocytosis that amoebae use, which is to say it turns its body into a terrifying mouth, like the *vagina dentata*, or toothed vagina, of folklore. Some killer cells of the immune system, more fastidiously, inject their prey with poisons and move on; others extrude extracellular threads that entrap and kill microbes. But the macrophage actually eats its prey, and this may give it a measure of independence unknown to most other body cells, which are totally dependent on the bloodstream for their nutrients.

Until recently, though, immunologists were far more interested in antibodies than in macrophages or any killer cells. Antibodies are the ingeniously bespoke protein molecules designed to bind to particular antigens—or patches of a microbe's surface—either disabling the microbe or marking it for destruction by macrophages. In the grand drama of antibody production—which was really the only drama in immunology once the molecular biologists seized center stage—macrophages were given only a minor supportive role. Their job was to "present" bits of foreign material (or antigens) to the presumably far cleverer white blood cells called lymphocytes that would manufacture the appropriate antibodies. As philosopher of science Emily Martin has pointed out, there is also a gender dimension to the derogation of macrophages, which have been described in the immunological literature as "housekeepers" and "little drudges."[2]

But here I must pause to confess that I am simplifying to an extent that would annoy many cellular immunologists. The alternative would be to descend into the dizzying detail of technical debates over the classification of cells. Some sources, for example, insist that the central antigen-presenting cells are not macrophages, but a related cell type called dendritic cells, which also arise in the bone marrow, and are also phagocytic.[3] Others argue that dendritic cells do not exist as a cell type separate from macrophages, pointing out that both these putative cell types possess the same chemical markers on their surfaces and react the same way to chemical growth factors in their environment.[4] More important, both types are capable of presenting antigens to lymphocytes and causing them to produce the appropriate antibodies, so that whether we call them macrophages, dendritic cells, or something more indecisive, they get the job done. This kind of taxonomic puzzle arises again and again in cellular immunology, where the mutability and mobility of individual cells constantly thwart rigid systems of classification. A macrophage, bursting with ingested material, in no way resembles a newly minted monocyte entering the bloodstream for the very first time.

The simplest system of classification is between the good guys and the bad guys—the latter being microbes and other threats to the body. Without any question, macrophages were the good guys, gobbling up microbes and often going on to help generate the production of antibodies that would coat any identical microbial invaders to make them even more appetizing to macrophages. How creative a role macrophages play in defense of the body—whether they are simply the cleanup crew or are more intimately involved in antibody production—is still not entirely clear. But to me as a lowly graduate student, they were heroes, always rushing out fearlessly to defend the body against microbes or other threats. They might be slow-witted compared to lymphocytes that produce antibodies, but they were in the vanguard of bodily defense.

Or so I thought until around the turn of the millennium, when some disturbing findings surfaced in the biomedical literature. Macrophages had been known since the nineteenth century to gather at tumor sites, leading Virchow and others to speculate that cancer is caused by inflammation, meaning a gathering of leucocytes at some site of injury or infection. Or, more optimistically, one might imagine that the macrophages were massing for an assault on the tumor. Instead, it turned out that they spent their time in the neighborhood of tumors encouraging the cancer cells to continue on their reproductive rampage. They are cheerleaders on the side of death. Frances Balkwill, one of the cell biologists who contributed to the recognition of treasonous macrophage behavior, described her colleagues in the field as being "horrified."[5]

By and large, medical science continues to present a happy face to the public. Self-help books and websites go right on advising cancer patients to boost their immune systems in order to combat the disease; patients should eat right and cultivate a supposedly immune-boosting "positive attitude." Better yet, they are urged to "visualize" the successful destruction of cancer cells by the body's immune cells, following guidelines such as:

- Cancer cells are weak and confused, and should be imagined as something that can fall apart like ground hamburger.
- There is an army of different kinds of white blood cells that can overwhelm the cancer cells.
- White blood cells are aggressive and want to seek out and attack the cancer cells.[6]

Philosophically, it is not easy to imagine one's own immune cells becoming accomplices in the deadly project of cancer, and denial has lingered on even in far more reputable venues than the self-help literature. In 2012 the distinguished physician and science writer Jerome Groopman wrote an entire article in the *New Yorker* on scientific attempts to enlist the immune system in fighting cancer without once mentioning that certain immune cells—macrophages—have a tendency to go over to the other side.[7] The omission is made all the stranger by the fact that Groopman introduces his essay with a story about a young woman in 1890 whose hand injury led to a long and painful inflammation, which was followed by a fatal metastatic sarcoma. In the article, he assures us, without explanation, that the sarcoma was "unrelated to her initial injury." By 2012, though, there had already been reports about the role of macrophages in injury-induced sarcomas.[8] Similarly, a 2016 *New York Times* article on "Harnessing the Immune System to Fight Cancer" makes no mention of macrophage treason.[9]

The evidence for macrophage collusion with cancer keeps piling up. Macrophages supply cancer cells with chemical growth factors and help build the new blood vessels required by a growing tumor. So intimately are they involved with the deadly progress of cancer that they can account for up to 50 percent of a tumor's mass. Macrophages also appear to be necessary if the cancer is to progress to its deadliest phase, metastasis, and if a cancerous mouse is treated to eliminate all its macrophages, the tumor stops metastasizing.[10]

Just in the last decade, scientists have begun to understand the perverse interaction that can lead macrophages and tumor cells to pool their resources and overwhelm the organism. The first part of the story can be expressed almost entirely in terms of chemistry. Any reasonably genteel meeting of two cells begins with an exchange of chemical messages, more or less like an exchange of business cards between two professionals, only in the cellular case the transaction can quickly get out of hand. As a 2014 article on breast cancer in the journal *Cancer Cell* suggests, the macrophages release a growth factor that encourages the cancer cells to elongate themselves into a mobile, invasive form poised for metastasis. These elongated cancer cells, in turn, release a chemical that further activates the macrophages—leading to the release of more growth factor, and so on. A positive feedback loop is established.[11] Or, to put it more colorfully, the macrophages and cancer cells seem to excite one another to the point where the cancer cells are pumped up and ready to set out from the breast in search of fresh territory to conquer—in the lungs, for example, or the liver or brain.

But describing the cellular interactions strictly in terms of the exchange of chemical messages is like trying to portray a human courtship as little more than an interaction of pheromones. For a more intimate view of what goes on between cells in the living body, we need to turn to the results of ingenious new techniques of microscopy capable of visualizing individual cells in the opaque environment of an active tumor. A kind of "intravital" microscopy, developed at John Condeelis's lab at the Albert Einstein College of Medicine, reveals that macrophages from within the tumor pair off with cancer cells to enter a blood vessel that would otherwise be impenetrable to the cancer cells. The macrophage has the chops, so to speak, to pry apart two adjacent blood vessel cells and make a hole through which the cancer cell can escape to colonize other parts of the body.[12] And the cancer cells are desperate to escape, since their own reproductive success creates a suffocatingly crowded environment within the tumor, dangerously short of oxygen. So it doesn't take just one rogue cell to create a metastatic cancer; it takes two—a cancer cell plus a normal, healthy, and all-too-helpful macrophage.

A science writer has to guard against overdramatizing and anthropomorphizing the events she is reporting on, but here the scientists involved have already done that for me. In 2015, two younger members of the Condeelis lab put together a short film showing the macrophage–tumor cell interactions that lead to breast cancer metastasis—both in animation and live footage of the microscopic events. The film begins with one of the narrators, a graduate student, wondering aloud, in an ominous tone, what genre of movie it belongs to: "horror…action…or war."[13] In his blog, the director of the National Institutes of Health likens the film to *Mission: Impossible* and writes almost breathlessly:

> Without giving *too* much of the plot away, let me just say that it involves cancer cells escaping from a breast tumor and spreading, or metastasizing, to other parts of the body. Along the way, those dastardly cancer cells take advantage of collagen fibers to make a tight-rope getaway and recruit key immune cells, called macrophages, to serve as double agents to aid and abet their diabolical spread.[14]

Breast cancer is not the only form of cancer that depends on macrophages for access to blood vessels and hence metastasis to new sites in the body. So far, there is evidence that macrophages assist in the metastasis of lung,[15] bone, gastric, and other cancers. And the macrophages' fiendish role in the growth of cancer does not end after they have escorted tumor cells into the bloodstream. Once at the remote site where the tumor cells have decided to settle, macrophages get to work on the job of angiogenesis— building new blood vessels to nourish the tumor.[16] (Whether the same macrophages that guide cancer cells into the bloodstream go on to do the work of angiogenesis is not known, at least as far as I can tell.)

Their complicity in cancer should be enough to disqualify macrophages as good guys, but that is not the only form of mischief that macrophages get into. Many pathological or at least annoying conditions, from acne to arthritis, arise from inflammation, and inflammation, which involves a variety of leucocytes, is spearheaded by macrophages. Acne, for example, is widely attributed to a bacterial infection, including by the manufacturers of a bactericidal cleanser called pHisohex, who advertise that their product will "Fight the bacteria, dirt and oil that bring on acne and pimples,"[17] although it is now well known that these ugly eruptions can occur in the absence of the bacterial suspects.[18] At a later phase in the human life cycle, we find macrophages involved in arthritis and diabetes, as well as chewing away at living bones to produce osteoporosis.

The blood vessels leading to the heart might be one of the last places you would expect to find errant immune cells, and for years the narrowing of these vessels—which can lead to heart attacks and strokes—was understood to be a result of fatty deposits along the arterial walls. Anyone seeking "heart health" was exhorted to eliminate saturated fat and cholesterol from their diet, if not all red meats and all forms of fat. "Atherosclerosis [narrowing of the cardiac arteries] was all about fats and grease," according to Peter Libby, a cardiologist and professor at Harvard Medical School. "Most physicians saw atherosclerosis as a straight plumbing problem."[19] Then came the discovery that the "bad" cholesterol in these arteries can trigger an inflammation that sets off strokes and heart attacks—another case, according to Libby, of "our body's defenses turned against ourselves."[20] Inflammation means an accumulation of macrophages, which a 2015 article asserts play "important roles in all stages of atherosclerosis."[21]

At this point, the emphasis on inflammation as a cause, if not *the* cause, of human ailments has achieved the dimensions of a fad. In a 2015 *New Yorker* article by Groopman (which is significant, among other things, for granting macrophages a status higher than janitors), he reports that "a growing number of doctors…believe that inflammation is the source of a wide range of conditions, including dementia, depression, autism, ADHD, and even aging."[22] It is no longer enough to eliminate fats and cholesterol from one's diet; an "anti-inflammatory diet" excludes processed foods, dairy products, and, commonly, meat. While such a diet may lead to weight loss, which can be a good thing, there is no hard evidence that it curbs inflammatory disorders or does anything else to tame the behavior of macrophages.[23]

One approach to the apparent unpredictability of macrophages is to abandon the category of "macrophages" and postulate that there are several subcategories of cells doing the various things we attribute to them. Supposedly, each category of macrophages has its own set of genetic instructions, which it obediently follows. For a while the favored division was between "M1 macrophages," which are responsible for killing microbes, and those of the "M2" variety, which focus on wound healing, but this classification does not account for the fact that the M2 designation "encompasses cells with dramatic differences in their biochemistry and physiology."[24] Or as one frustrated team of researchers put it, "Instead of having a finite number of variants that can be easily counted, we have an infinite number of polarized [activated] macrophages."[25] A common response has been to double down on the functional classification of macrophages, as a 2008 article proposes:

We suggest that a more informative foundation for macrophage classification should be based on the fundamental macrophage functions that are involved in maintaining homeostasis [a state of balance supposedly necessary for the health of the organism]. We propose three such functions: host defence, wound healing and immune regulation.[26]

But what about macrophages' role in abetting cancer—or in instigating life-threatening inflammatory diseases? What "functions" do these activities represent? As it turns out, the macrophages that launch tumor cells into the bloodstream do not seem to fit either canonical category M1 or M2,[27] suggesting that we should be focusing less on static categories than on the mutability of individual macrophages. Maybe, crazy as it sounds, they are not following any kind of "instructions," but doing what they feel like doing.

CHAPTER NINE

Tiny Minds

Well before the twentieth-century triumph of the molecular biologists, the whole field of immunology had begun with the close observation of individual macrophages. Observation is usually the job of naturalists, who crouch patiently in the bushes to study, for example, the behavior of wild animals. Laboratory scientists are more prone to aggressive interventions, which might involve chopping up the animals' brains and studying their biochemical composition. Fortunately, the "father" of cellular biology had both the patience of a naturalist and the intellectual impatience of an ambitious lab researcher.

The brilliant and obsessive Russian zoologist Elie Metchnikoff, who was described in Paul de Kruif's 1926 book *Microbe Hunters* as being "like some hysterical character out of one of Dostoyevski's novels,"[1] had been attracted to macrophages while studying flatworms and sponges. Macrophages are eye-catching enough—large cells capable of moving among other body cells—and as he was the first to discover, they had an even better trick: They could ingest

particles (such as microbes) by enfolding them and expos-
ing them to powerful digestive enzymes, the process that
Metchnikoff named phagocytosis. The question was how
the macrophages knew what to attack and what to leave
alone, which cells or particles were "normal" and which
were deserving of destruction. Metchnikoff's answer was
essentially that macrophages, enjoying the "most independence" of any body cells, could decide this on their own[2]—
protecting cells they recognized as belonging to the "self"
and devouring anything else.

This explanation was instantly rejected by most of
Metchnikoff's contemporaries. As philosopher Alfred
Tauber writes, "The phagocyte [macrophage] as possessor
of its own destiny and mediator of the organism's selfhood
was received as too vitalistic a conception,"[3] meaning that
it was almost mystical. How could a microscopic cell make
decisions? On the one hand it was too small and, of course,
utterly lacking anything resembling a nervous system. On
the other hand it was too large, at least compared to the
individual molecules increasingly favored by twentieth-
century molecular biologists as the arbiters of everything
that goes on in the body. And what is a cell anyway except a
collection of proteins, lipids, nucleic acids, and other chemicals enclosed in a lipid-based membrane? When, during a
phone interview in 2016, I asked Alberto Mantovani, one
of the early researchers on the role of macrophages in tumor development, what he thought of the growing interest
in "cellular decision making," he asked me to repeat the
phrase. Then he guffawed.

But there it is: A little over a century after Metchnikoff's dismissal for the scientific crime of "vitalism," the forbidden phrase began to gain respectability. I say "a little over a century" because I cannot locate its first appearance in the scientific literature. By 2005 the term "cellular decision making"— without the quotation marks—was showing up in the titles of articles; five years later it was the subject of international conferences. Why Mantovani was unaware of it I do not know and was perhaps too polite to ask. I will admit, though, that even to me the notion still carries a whiff of whimsy.

Officially, cellular decision making is "the process whereby cells assume different, functionally important and heritable fates without an associated genetic or environmental difference."[4] One translation would be "a process that we do not understand and cannot predict." For mobile cells like macrophages and amoebae, one of the most common decisions is about where to go next, and here we humans can only make large generalizations—such as that they will move toward edible or otherwise attractive material. But this is a very general observation. New techniques, like intravital microscopy, have made it possible to track the behavior of individual cells in living tissue, and the resulting images reveal striking degrees of individuality. If you calculate the bulk average of movements within a sample group of cells, most cells turn out to be going their own way, on paths far from the average.[5] Cancer cells within a tumor exhibit "extreme diversity."[6] NK, or "natural killer," cells, which, like macrophages, attack targets like microbes, do not always kill. A 2013 article reports that about half of the NK cells sit out the fight, leaving a minority of them to become what their human observers call "serial killers."[7]

Another type of immune cell, the T cells or thymus-derived lymphocytes that are attacked by the HIV virus, are especially frustrating to observers because they move about

> by a series of repetitive lunges, repeatedly balling-up and then extending. This cycle appears to be driven by an intrinsic rhythmicity, with a period of about 2 min....T cells travel in a fairly consistent direction during each "lunge" and may even continue in a consistent direction over several cycles. However, following each pause, there is a high probability that a cell will take off in another direction.[8]

The fact that something is not completely predictable does not mean that it is unexplainable. As one explanation for cellular motion, scientists offer "stochastic noise," meaning that cells are being randomly jostled by other cells (or particles in the extracellular fluid). In any fluid or gas, the molecules are in motion at speeds determined by the temperature. Sometimes they collide with each other and rebound in new directions, which can create the impression of self-determined motion. The other type of explanation is that some of the particles or molecules colliding with cells are not entirely "random," because they contain information encoded as chemical messages. For example, macrophages and other immune cells use small proteins called cytokines to summon others of their kind for help at a site of inflammation. So, a determined determinist might say, cells are not "deciding" what to do, they are being told what to do.

But the experiences of being randomly jostled and, perhaps at the same time, receiving intelligible messages are also common to the only creatures who insist on possessing "free will"—ourselves. While walking on a sidewalk, I may collide, apparently randomly, with other pedestrians, and in ways that cause me to walk closer to or farther from the curb. At the same time, I may be receiving text messages on my phone advising me to hurry up or to not forget to pick up some groceries. All of this incoming data—the crowded sidewalk, the shopping list—must be processed by my mind before I can decide on the best direction and speed at which to walk. There may be additional factors that would make me alter my path. If, for example, I am trying to avoid someone else in the crowd, I might suddenly speed up and slip around a corner. The differences between a human being negotiating a busy sidewalk and a single cell are of course almost unfathomably large. A cell is a cell; a human is composed of trillions of cells—enough so that a trillion or so can be dedicated to collecting and parsing information from the environment. But second by second, both the individual cell and the conglomeration of cells we call a "human" are doing the same thing: processing incoming data and making decisions.

I learned an important lesson in nonhuman decision making from my own crude informal form of birdwatching. While living on the Gulf side of the lower Florida Keys, I became intrigued by the group behavior of ibises. As the sun set, they would flock to a nearby mangrove island to roost for the night; sometime around sunrise they would take off again for their feeding grounds. I assumed that both events were driven by the angle and intensity of the sunlight or perhaps by some ibis leaders or central committee. How else would the birds know what to do? But further observations revealed that the morning liftoff could be the coordinated action of up to a hundred birds at a time, or it could be messy and anarchic, with individuals and small groups taking off at slightly different times. When I asked an animal behaviorist—an old friend at Cornell—what was controlling their behavior, he did not rule out the effect of the sun or the possible existence of trendsetters among the ibises, but suggested that there was a lot of early morning jostling and nudging. In other words, nothing was "controlling" them in the determinist sense I was looking for, no on/off switch telling the birds to stay put or get up and forage. Inadvertently, I had stumbled across what has been called the Harvard law of animal behavior, which is related to Murphy's law: "You can have the most beautifully designed experiment with the most carefully controlled variables, and the animal will do what it damn well pleases."[9]

It had not occurred to me, with my PhD in cell biology, that a truly "bird-brained" creature like an ibis could be making any decisions at all, either individually or collectively, just as it had not occurred to me that the actions of individual cells were not fully determined by the cells' environments and genes. But much smaller biological entities than bird brains have been credited with "decision making." In 2007, a German team discovered what they called "free will" among, of all things, fruit flies. The flies were immobilized by tethering them and gluing them to the inside of an all-white drum that offered no sensory clues. Still, the tormented flies struggled desperately to fly, with the humans all the while recording their motions and subjecting them to a variety of mathematical analyses. The result was that the flies' motions were not random, as mathematically defined; they were spontaneous and originated in the insects themselves.[10] And why would a fruit fly want to generate nonrandom but completely unpredictable patterns of motion? According to Bjorn Brembs, the leader of the team, unpredictability could confer a survival advantage: A more "deterministically" designed type of creature—say, one that always moves to the right when alarmed—would be far more susceptible to predators.

One criticism Brembs reported from a neurobiologist colleague was that fruit flies are simply "too small" to engage in decision making, much less anything as exalted as "free will." But they are far from the smallest specks of living or life-like material to exhibit autonomous behavior. Perhaps one of the examples best known to biologists is the phage lambda, a virus that preys on that familiar resident of our guts—the bacterium *E. coli*. A virus is a strand or two of nucleic acid, usually DNA, coated with protein, visible only through an electron microscope, yet in the course of their development phage have a crucial choice to make: When one of them penetrates an *E. coli* cell, it can either remain there in a state of dormancy, passively reproducing its nucleic acid when the cell divides, or it can immediately *lyse* the cell—splitting it open and releasing a swarm of progeny to invade other *E. coli*. Acres of paper have been filled with differential equations in an effort to predict which way an encounter between phage and *E. coli* will go, with the result that the outcome seems to depend on decision making by individual phage.[11]

As we proceed down the scale—from cells to molecules

and from molecules to atoms and subatomic particles—the level of spontaneity only increases until we reach the wild dance party that goes on at the quantum level. Quantum physics has shown that the behavior of subatomic particles is inherently unpredictable. For example, when a beam of electrons is passed through a pair of slits, each electron gets to "choose" which one to enter. It is impossible, in the case of an atom or subatomic particle, to simultaneously know where it is and how fast it is going. As the renowned physicist Freeman Dyson has put it, "There is a certain kind of freedom that atoms have to jump around, and they seem to choose entirely on their own without any input from the outside, so in a certain sense atoms have free will."[12]

Such statements come with an implicit disclaimer: No one is implying that cells or viruses or subatomic particles possess consciousness, desires, or personalities. What they possess is *agency*, or the ability to initiate an action. If even that seems like a reckless statement, it is because we are so unused to thinking of agency as an attribute of anything other than humans, or God, or perhaps some of the larger "charismatic" animals, like elephants or whales. I am using the word in the generous philosophical sense employed by Jessica Riskin in her brilliant book *The Restless Clock* as "something like consciousness but more basic, more rudimentary, a primitive, prerequisite quality. A thing cannot be conscious without having agency, but it can have agency without being conscious."[13] Agency, she goes on, is "simply an intrinsic capacity to act in the world, to do things in a way that is neither predetermined nor random."[14] We routinely and colloquially ascribe agency to things we know are not conscious or even alive, as in, "This car just doesn't want to start," fully realizing that the car doesn't "want" anything. Riskin's point is that the mission of science—the determinist science that arose in the middle of the seventeenth century—has been the elimination of the last vestiges of agency from the natural world. Lightning, we are told, is an electrical charge, not an expression of divine displeasure. The amoeba does not move because it "wants" to, but because it is driven by chemical gradients in its environment. Tell a scientifically trained person that something is unpredictable and she will do her best to find a way to predict and control it. But agency is not concentrated in humans or their gods or favorite animals. It is dispersed throughout the universe, right down to the smallest imaginable scale.

Science has an answer to Riskin's thesis. According to the latest from the field of cognitive science, humans have an innate tendency to see agency, whether in the form of gods or spirits, where it does not exist because there was once a survival advantage in doing so. A prehistoric person or hominid would be wise to imagine that every stirring in the tall grass meant that a leopard—or some such potentially hazardous life form—was closing in for an attack. If you decide the stirring is a leopard, you can run away, and if you were wrong, nothing is lost except perhaps some temporary peace of mind. But if you decide that it is just a breeze and it turns out to be a leopard, you become a leopard's lunch. So our brains evolved to favor the scarier alternative and the choice of running. We have become what the cognitive scientists call "hyperactive agency detection devices": We see faces in clouds, hear denunciations in thunder, and sense conscious beings all around us even when there is nothing there. This has become a key part of the scientific argument against religion, and one of the best-known books on the subject is entitled *Why Would Anyone Believe in God?*

If it seems a rather precipitous leap from imagined leopards to monotheistic deities, this may be because the cognitive scientists made it too quickly. The point is not that many of the leopards turned out *not* to be there, but that in the world occupied by hominids and early humans, they often were. Quite possibly many of our ancestors knew full well they were erring on the side of caution and made the error anyway, which is a choice we can understand. What may be harder for us to understand today is that we evolved on a planet densely occupied by other "agents"—animals that could destroy us with the slash of a claw or the splash of a fin, arbitrarily and in seconds. The hypothesized transition from suspected predators to the morally ambiguous "spirits" believed in by early humans makes more sense when we recall that, before humans could hunt for themselves, they seem to have relied on the bones and scraps of meat left by nonhuman predators. That is, the predator was also a provider, more or less like the gods that came later.

The scientific argument, in other words, is that the attribution of agency to the natural word was a mistake, although a useful one in an evolutionary sense. I am suggesting, to the contrary, that it was the notion of nature as a passive, ultimately inert mechanism that was the mistake, and perhaps the biggest one that humans ever made. The "death of nature," as Carolyn Merchant put it, turned the natural world from a companionable, though often threatening place, into a resource to be exploited.[15] Determined to reduce biology to chemistry, twentieth-century biologists tended to skip right over life at the cellular level; molecules were much more manageable and far more predictable than living cells. In doing so, though, biology generated paradoxes and mysteries, like the problem of immune cells that abet cancer or foment autoimmune diseases. Through the lens of reductionist science, even life itself became a kind of mystery, resolvable only as an incredibly complex concatenation of molecular events. Today we tend to accord the status of "mystery" to something that should be as intimately familiar as life, and that is consciousness.

If there is a lesson here it has to do with humility. For all our vaunted intelligence and "complexity," we are not the sole authors of our destinies or of anything else. You may exercise diligently, eat a medically fashionable diet, and still die of a sting from an irritated bee. You may be a slim, toned paragon of wellness, and still a macrophage within your body may decide to throw in its lot with an incipient tumor. Elie Metchnikoff understood this as well as any biologist since his time ever has. Rejecting the traditional—and continuing—themes of harmony and wholeness, he posited a biology based on conflict *within* the body and carried on by the body's own cells as they compete for space and food and oxygen. We may influence the outcome of these conflicts—through our personal habits and perhaps eventually through medical technologies that will persuade immune cells to act in more responsible ways—but we cannot control it. And we certainly cannot forestall its inevitable outcome, which is death.

CHAPTER TEN

"Successful Aging"

The pressure to remain fit, slim, and in control of one's body does not end with old age—in fact, it only grows more insistent. Friends, family members, and doctors start nagging the aging person to join a gym, "eat healthy," or, at the very least, go for daily walks. You may have imagined a reclining chair or a hammock awaiting you after decades of stress and, in the case of manual laborers, physical exertion. But no, your future more likely holds a treadmill and a lat pull, at least if you can afford to access these devices. One of the bossier self-help books for seniors commands:

> *Exercise six days a week for the rest of your life.* Sorry, but that's it. No negotiations. No give. No excuses. Six days, serious exercise, until you die.[1]

The reason for this draconian regime is that "once you pass the age of fifty, exercise is no longer optional. You have to exercise or get old." You may have retired from paid work, but you have a new job, going to the gym. "Think of it as a great job, which it is."[2]

People over fifty-five are now the fastest-growing demographic for gym membership. A few gyms, like the Silver Sneakers chain, deliberately target the elderly, in some cases even to the point of discouraging those who are younger— on the theory that older folks don't want to be intimidated by meatballs or spandexed sylphs. If the mere presence of white-haired gym-goers isn't enough to repel the young, some gyms don't offer free weights, partly because the sound of falling weights is supposedly annoying to older people and partly because older people, who are more likely to use exercise machines, may see them as a reproach. In the mixed-age gym I go to, membership tilts toward the over-fifty crowd, where "exercise is no longer optional." The more dedicated may use the gym as only part of their fitness regimen; they run in the morning or bike several miles to get there. Mark, a fifty-eight-year-old white-collar worker, does a 6 a.m. workout before going to work, then another one after work. His goal? "To keep going." The price of survival is endless toil.

For an exemplar of healthy aging, we are often referred to Jeanne Louise Calment, a Frenchwoman who died in 1997 at the age of 122—the longest confirmed human life span.[3] Calment never worked in her life, but it could be said she "worked out." While he was still alive, she and her wealthy husband enjoyed tennis, swimming, fencing, hunting, and mountaineering. She took up fencing when she was 85, and even at 111, when she was in a nursing home, started the morning with gymnastics performed in her wheelchair.

Anyone looking for dietary tips will be disappointed; she liked beef, fried foods, chocolates, and pound cake. Unthinkably, by today's standards, she smoked cigarettes and sometimes cigars, though antismoking advocates should be relieved to know that she suffered from a persistent cough in her final years.

This is "successful aging," which, except for the huge investment of time it can require, is almost indistinguishable from not aging at all. Anthropologist Sarah Lamb and her coauthors of a book on the subject[4] date the concept of successful aging to the 1980s and locate it throughout the Western world, where it also goes by such names as "active aging," "healthy aging," "productive aging," "vital aging," "anti-aging," and "aging well."[5] Lamb reports that

> the WHO dedicated World Health Day 2012 to Healthy Ageing, and the European Union designated 2012 as the European Year for Active Ageing.[6] In North America and Western Europe, centers for Healthy Aging, Active Aging and Successful Aging abound. Popular cultural and self-help books on the topic are flourishing.[7]

Among the titles now available on Amazon are: *Successful and Healthy Aging: 101 Best Ways to Feel Younger and Live Longer*; *Live Long, Die Short: A Guide to Authentic Health and Successful Aging*; *Do Not Go Gentle: Successful Aging for Baby Boomers and All Generations*; *Aging Backwards: Reverse the Aging Process and Look 10 Years Younger in 30 Minutes a Day*; and of course *Healthy Aging for Dummies*. A major theme is that aging itself is abnormal and unacceptable. As the physician coauthor of *Younger Next Year* wrote, under the subhead " 'Normal Aging' Isn't Normal":

> The more I looked at the science, the more it became clear to me that such ailments and deterioration [heart attacks, strokes, the common cancers, diabetes, most falls, fractures] are *not* a normal part of growing old. They are an outrage.[8]

And who is responsible for this outrage? Well, each of us is individually responsible. All of the books in the successful-aging literature insist that a long and healthy life is within the reach of anyone who will submit to the required discipline. It's up to you and you alone, never mind what scars—from overexertion, genetic defects, or poverty—may be left from your prior existence. Nor is there much or any concern for the material factors that influence the health of an older person, such as personal wealth or access to transportation and social support. Except for your fitness trainer or successful-aging guru, you're on your own.

Unfortunately, the gurus' instructions are far from unanimous or easy to follow. On the dietary front there's no more clarity than can be found in the general dietary advice for adults. Should you go with a Paleo diet or one heavy in complex carbohydrates? Should you eliminate all fats that do not originate in avocados or olives? We are widely advised to follow a "Mediterranean diet," but does that include Greek gyros and Italian charcuterie? Or perhaps we should refrain from eating anything at all. Numerous studies have shown that caloric restriction or intermittent fasting can prolong the lives of rats and other animals, but the debate over its effectiveness in humans goes on,[9] despite the fact that most of us would find a semi-starved life not worth living. If I can discern a general rule, it is governed by deprivation: Anything you like to eat—because it is, for example, fatty, salty, or sweet—should probably be put aside now in the interests of successful aging.

As for exercise, here too we find no precise instructions. Some sources, like the book quoted above, specify the rough amount of exercise, such as six days a week for about forty-five minutes per session, and how it should be divided between cardiovascular work and muscle training. But overall, a disturbing vagueness prevails. Often, we are urged simply to "get active" or "get moving," on the grounds that even the smallest motion can be life-prolonging. "And even if you can't run a four-minute mile, keep running. If you can't run, walk—but keep moving."[10] For the sedentary, fidgeting at one's desk can help, along with parking a block or so from one's destination. A middle-aged woman reports that "I keep maniacally active because if there's any down time I sit there feeling guilty I'm not doing anything."[11] Not doing anything is the same as aging; health and longevity must be earned through constant activity. Even the tremors of Parkinson's disease can be seen, optimistically, as a form of health-giving exercise, since they do, after all, burn calories. The one thing you should not be doing is sitting around and, say, reading a book about healthy aging.

There are bright sides to aging, such as declines in ambition, competitiveness, and lust. In her seventies, Betty Friedan turned her attention from gender to aging, writing a book called *The Fountain of Age* and telling an interviewer that as they age, people become "more and more authentically themselves. They didn't care anymore what other people thought of them, you know, keeping up with the Joneses and 'Am I going to make a fool of myself?'"[12] Another noted feminist, the Australian-born Englishwoman Lynne Segal, found artists often doing their best work in old age, and titled her balanced and richly documented book *Out of Time: The Pleasures and Perils of Ageing*. I can add from my own experience that aging also comes along with a refreshing refusal to strive, to take on every potential obligation and opportunity that comes my way.

But as even the most ebullient of the elderly eventually comes to realize aging is above all an accumulation of disabilities, often beginning well before Medicare eligibility or the arrival of the first Social Security check. Vision loss typically begins in one's forties, bringing the need for reading glasses. Menopause strikes in a woman's early fifties, along with the hollowing out of bones. Knee and lower back pain arise in the forties and fifties, compromising the mobility required for "successful aging." As we older people mutter to each other in the gym, "It's just one damn thing after another," most of these things are too commonplace and boring even to serve as small talk. The U.S. Census Bureau reports that nearly 40 percent of people age sixty-five and older suffer from at least one disability, with two-thirds of them saying they have difficulty walking or climbing.[13] Yet we soldier along, making occasional concessions to arthritic joints or torn muscles but always aware that any major cessation of effort, say for two weeks or more, could lead to catastrophic collapse. "You don't become inactive because you age," we've been told over and over. "You age because you've become inactive."

No doubt immortality would be a more alluring goal if we could imagine surviving without disability, but hardly anyone, outside of the narrow demographic slice represented by Silicon Valley billionaires, is interested in an extended life of being fed and "toileted" by caretakers until the next biomedical breakthrough comes along. More modestly, the goal of "successful aging" is often described as a "compression of morbidity" into one's last few years. In other words, a healthy, active life followed by a swift descent into death. The latter goal may help account for the rise of "extreme" and dangerous sports in recent years, at least among those who can afford ski resorts, snowboarding, or a trip to Nepal. While the poor are chided for unhealthy lifestyles, the rich are applauded for summiting Everest, an enterprise with a 6.5 percent mortality rate[14] and costing a minimum of about $100,000, not counting equipment or airfare—although fitness enthusiasts will be happy to know that both gluten-free and vegan diets are now available to climbers.[15]

But the goals of a healthy, active life followed by a fairly quick death may not even be compatible without the intervention of avalanches and altitude sickness. The truly sinister possibility is that for many of us, all the little measures we take to remain fit—all the deprivations and exertions—will only lead to a longer chance to live with crippling and humiliating disabilities. As a *New York Times* columnist observed, "The price we're paying for extended life spans is a high rate of late-life disability."[16] There are no guarantees.

But where there are no guarantees, there are plenty of

promises, of which "younger next year" is far from the most extravagant. Skincare products, once content to be "age-defying," are increasingly claimed to be "age-reversing," and, we are told by the wellness coaches and websites, a youthful appearance is part of "feeling good about yourself," which is deemed essential to wellness at any chronological age. Credit for adding beauty—or at least a simulacrum of youthfulness—to the wellness package should go to the new "celebrity wellness" entrepreneurs, starting with actor Gwyneth Paltrow, whose digital company Goop has been dispensing tips on beauty, health, recipes, and shopping since 2008. Actor Blake Lively launched her own "lifestyle company" in 2013, which is about "living a very one-of-a-kind, curated life," and included home decorating tips.[17]

The general assumption is that the customers have plenty of time and money on their hands for, among many other things, a $60 "skin-rejuvenating pillowcase with patented Copper technology," or a $5,000 "radiofrequency" skin-tightening treatment. If you have enough money for such gadgets and interventions, you can presumably buy your way out of the strenuous "younger next year" approach to aging and take a more sybaritic path, one designed not to challenge but to pamper. The celebrity wellness entrepreneur du jour, Amanda Bacon, who is a celebrity only by virtue of her Moon Juice wellness products, offers, instead of exercise regimens, a line of ointments and drinks, heavy on the kinds of exotic and expensive substances that Bacon herself likes to consume: "ho shou wu, silver needle tea, pearl, reishi, cordyceps, quinton shots, bee pollen and chaga." The theme here is self-nurturance, as reflected in the cost of the items consumed, as well as the time that goes into "curating" and procuring them. As *New York Times* reporter Molly Young comments:

> What Goop (and acolytes like Moon Juice) sell is the notion that it's not only excusable but worthy for a person to spend hours a day focused on her tiniest mood shifts, food choices, beauty rituals, exercise habits, bathing routines and sleep schedule. What they sell is self-absorption as the ultimate luxury product.[18]

Not surprisingly, these celebrity-endorsed wellness techniques are not exactly evidence-based, although of course there may be some large-scale double-blind randomized studies of, say, the salubrious effects of pearl consumption, that I am not aware of. But there are other equally passive and sweat-free wellness techniques that claim slightly more scientific credibility, such as "touch therapy." It is known that human infants and probably those of many other mammals only thrive when held and touched. Extrapolating from that, some wellness purveyors surmise that even adults in modern societies suffer from "touch deprivation"—most of all the elderly ones, who may have lost, or lost interest in, their partners and simply aged out of the dating pool.

Fortunately, touch is easy enough to commoditize in the form of massages or "healing touch" therapies that can be offered by spas, hospitals, and senior care centers. An assisted living center excitedly tells us that touch reduces blood pressure and glucose and increases alertness, while all-out hugs "strengthen the immune system, relieve pain and depression, elevate mood, reduce stress, decrease the heart rate, and may prevent Parkinson's disease."[19] The hugs can be dispensed by care providers or acquired from the fledgling "cuddling industry," which offers asexual cuddles for a price.[20]

Inflammaging

In the twentieth century, medical science began to think of aging as a kind of disease as opposed to a normal stage of the life cycle. Women were used to having their lives "medicalized" from puberty to menopause, with pregnancy and childbirth as acute episodes requiring intense medical monitoring and often intervention. But since there was no cure for aging, the elderly were pretty much left to their own devices, once meaning tonics and elixirs rich in alcohol or cocaine, which may have been, at least in the short term, highly effective. Not until the 1960s and '70s did a researcher come up with a theory of aging at the subcellular level, which in the reductionist biology of the time was the only level that counted as interesting. This was the "telomere theory": Every time a cell divides, the tips of its chromosomes (telomeres) grow shorter until further cell divisions become impossible.

The theory had its problems—many types of cells, such as cardiac cells and neurons, do not reproduce or do not do so very often, yet they somehow manage to age. But it also presented a tempting commercial opportunity in the form of drugs that might lengthen and fortify telomeres, although their pharmaceutical promise has not been fulfilled. A host of other chemical agents in the aging process have been identified, each with its own proposed nostrum. Free radicals were popular culprits in the 1980s and '90s, leading to a brief fad of consuming antioxidants like vitamin E and selenium—to no effect, as it turned out. Methylation, the addition of a methyl group to a protein or nucleic acid, is required for cellular health and is thought to be encouraged by B vitamins such as folate. But the effect of B vitamins on aging is murky at best.[21] Or, it has been proposed, mutations can occur in a cell's DNA, leading to accumulated intracellular damage, and there is no known cure for that.

All of these proposed chemical pathways of aging occur within individual cells, and all are suggestive of the kind of deep trends one might associate with aging—decay and entropy. The analogy is often made to the kind of "wear and tear" that eventually disables a machine or at least its moving parts, except that cells are not machines and their moving parts are molecules or clusters of molecules that are subject to perpetual destruction and renewal. Proteins, the fundamental chemical ingredient of cells, are constantly being torn apart by intracellular digestive enzymes and replaced by freshly constructed ones. Some of the key protein players in cellular metabolism have half-lives only minutes long, meaning that there are plenty of opportunities for errors, as well as opportunities for correcting them. Over time, though, with advancing age, the errors accumulate until the integrity of the cell is compromised. And it is then that things get interesting.

Damaged cells attract immune cells, or, more precisely,

damaged cells send out chemical signals that attract the immune cells, which proceed to devour the ailing cells. Some of the immune cells are messy eaters, leaving behind debris or the equivalent of crumbs, which in turn attracts more immune cells. Macrophages in particular are drawn to damaged cells; in fact, their chief "function" in the body, in addition to fighting microbes, is the removal of such compromised cells. Thus the site of cell damage becomes a site of inflammation, where macrophages pile up and attract more macrophages to share in the meal. Inflammation is of course lifesaving when provoked by microbes, but when the target is the body's own cells or damaged versions thereof, it can lead, however gradually, to death.

In 2000, the Italian immunologist Claudio Franceschi proposed the neologism "inflammaging" to describe the entire organism-wide process of aging. Far from being a simple process of decay originating in individual cells, aging involves the active mobilization of macrophages to deal with proliferating sites of cellular damage. Today Franceschi's theory is widely accepted, with inflammaging being described, ominously enough, as "chronic smoldering oxidative and inflammatory stress."[22] The hallmark disorders of aging—such as atherosclerosis, arthritis, Alzheimer's disease, diabetes, and osteoporosis—are all inflammatory diseases, characterized by a local buildup of macrophages. In atherosclerosis, for example, macrophages settle in the arteries leading to the heart, where they gorge themselves with lipids until the arteries are eventually blocked. In Type 2 diabetes macrophages accumulate in the pancreas, where they destroy the cells that produce insulin. Osteoporosis involves the activation of bone-dwelling macrophages, called osteo-clasts, that kill normal bone cells. The inflammation associ-ated with Alzheimer's disease was first thought to represent macrophages' attempts to control the beta-amyloid plaques that clog up the Alzheimer's brain. But the most recent re-search suggests that the macrophages, which may indeed be activated by the plaques, actually drive the progression of the disease.[23]

These are not "degenerative" diseases, not just accumula-tions of "errors" and cobwebs. They are active and seeming-ly purposeful attacks by the immune system on the body itself. Why should this happen? Perhaps a better question is: Why shouldn't it happen? The survival of an older per-son is of no evolutionary consequence since that person can no longer reproduce—unless one wants to argue for the role of grandparents in prolonging the lives of their de-scendants. It might even, in a Darwinian sense, be better to remove the elderly before they can use up any more resources that might otherwise go to the young. In that case, you could say that there is something almost altruistic about the diseases of aging. Just as programmed cell death, apoptosis, cleanly eliminates damaged cells from the body, so do the diseases of aging clear up the clutter of biologi-cally useless older people—only not quite so cleanly. And this perspective may be particularly attractive at a time, like now, when the dominant discourse on aging focuses on the deleterious economic effects of largely aging populations. If we didn't have inflammatory diseases to get the job done, we might have to turn to euthanasia.

But however benevolent the diseases of aging might ultimately be—at least from a social or economic perspective—they are experienced by the individual as a betrayal. In one of his last novels, *Everyman*, Philip Roth's protagonist, who is essentially the same Rothlike, sex-obsessed character who has starred in most of his novels, must face his own physical deterioration. Well into his seventies, retired and largely estranged from his family, he is still hitting on women at least a half century younger than himself. Mostly though, he is aging—tormented by his increasingly unreliable penis and by atherosclerosis, which comes to require heart surgery every year. The setting is increasingly claustrophobic as it moves among waiting rooms and hospitals before returning to the cemetery where the story started, at a family funeral, and where his own body will eventually rest. It is unlikely that Roth knew anything about inflammaging or the cellular basis of atherosclerosis, but he accurately summed up the biological situation when he wrote that "old age isn't a battle; old age is a massacre."[24]

So whatever good deeds immune cells may accomplish in the young, such as fending off microbial infections, their job—or perhaps we should say, their effect in the elderly—is to destroy the organism. The question of why they do these things might be simplified into a more childish form: Are the immune cells "good" or are they "bad"? Friends or foes? For the most part, scientists dodge this question with mumblings about "paradoxical" effects or a "double-edged sword." Macrophages can save our lives or promote deadly tumors. Neutrophils, which are among the first immune cells to arrive at a site of infection, can slay intruders or start a spiral into chronic inflammation. Scientists sometimes fall back on the language of moral judgment, of "good" and "bad." For example, a researcher who has contributed to several papers on inflammation attempts to exonerate neutrophils by blaming their occasional bad behavior on other cell types they are in contact with, which are typically other immune cells:

> Although neutrophils may often appear to be the "bad" guy in certain inflammatory conditions this is typically due to the influence of other molecules released from surrounding cells. Without this influence the primary aim of the neutrophil is to resolve inflammation, making them overall the "good" guys of the inflammatory process.[25]

It would take a lengthy trial to determine the guilt or innocence of the immune system or of any cell type within it. In the case of macrophages their contributions to the well-being of the organism are well known: They help sculpt the embryo into a human fetus; they defend the body against microbial invasions; they participate in the process of antigen presentation; they keep the body clear of dead and damaged cells. On the destructive side, they encourage the growth and spread of tumors; they launch the catastrophe of inflammaging; they are frontline killers in autoimmune diseases. If I were a prosecutor in the trial of macrophages I might wind up my case with the autoimmune diseases, which may not prove active malice on the macrophages' part, but certainly make a case for homicidal negligence. In their defense, macrophages could argue that whatever the deleterious consequences, they are simply doing the kind of things they are expected to do—removing damaged cells, for example. To which the prosecution might counter that macrophages have way too much discretion in determining which cells are damaged enough to die, and may even have caused the initial harm themselves.

Early in his massive work on the history and philosophy of immunology, *The Immune Self: Theory or Metaphor*, Alfred Tauber states that "the immune self has come to be viewed analogously to a living entity."[26] His use of the passive voice conceals *who* has come to see the "immune self" in this way—he himself or immunologists in general? But the larger question is, what does it mean to say that some part or parts of the body act as a "living entity"? Certainly the cells of the immune system are in constant communication, and are capable of rather dramatic forms of cooperation. For example, if a macrophage needs to expand its supply of cell-killing digestive enzymes, all it has to do is gobble up a neutrophil and add the neutrophil's stockpile of enzymes to its own. So the immune system seems to qualify as a "system," but does it possess the autonomy we expect to find in a "living entity"? If so, we should probably call the nervous system a kind of living entity too, since it is capable of plotting and carrying out the death of the organism—in the form of suicide by gunshot or poison—on its own.

But what kind of an entity is it? Is it a second, shadow self, assuming the word "self" has not been so degraded by its metaphorical uses as to be meaningless? The best analogy I can come up with would be that it is a symbiont—living in a symbiotic relationship within us, sometimes saving our lives and sometimes destroying us. All we can say for sure is that its agenda does not always concur with ours, and there does not seem to be any command-and-control center within the organism to bring these agendas reliably into harmony. There are many small measures, to be sure—checks and balances, anti- and pro-inflammatory chemical messages—but there is ultimately no one in charge.

The danger is that the inflammatory forays of the immune system can easily tilt into lethal cascades. A plaque composed of macrophages can suddenly block a coronary artery. Alzheimer's disease, which is an inflammatory disease of the brain, can cut off the neuronal circuits controlling breathing. Where there is an inflammation, body cells are damaged, and the damage lures more inflammatory cells to the site. Macrophages get less efficient with age, slower and less effective as phagocytes and defenders against microbial invasions. But the effect may be to make them even messier eaters than they were in their youth, and hence more prone to inadvertently call for more macrophages as backup. Chronic, "smoldering" inflammations can easily ignite into conflagrations.

We all know how this ends, though for the most part we prefer not to think about it. When the organism dies, as signaled by the cessation of the heartbeat and respiration, not all body cells die simultaneously, though many begin to ail within minutes or hours. Their mitochondria swell, their disabled proteins are not replaced, their cell membranes start to leak. Macrophages and other phagocytes, which are not wholly dependent on the bloodstream for nutrients, may last slightly longer and perhaps enjoy a brief orgy as they rush around devouring damaged cells, but they too soon succumb to the lack of oxygen from circulating blood. Bacteria from the gut—collectively known as the microbiome—find their way through leaky membranes to the rest of the body and begin the process of putrefaction. Next come the insects, including beetles, flies, and, should they be in the neighborhood, butterflies. Maggots are the hallmark of decomposition; Shakespeare remarked that "we fat [fatten] ourselves for maggots" and was amused by the fact that even kings are eventually eaten by these little worms. Mercifully perhaps, the corpse may be attacked at some point by larger scavengers—crows, vultures, rats, hyenas, jackals, and dogs—which at least serve to clean up the mess. To the heroes of the *Iliad*, this was the ultimate humiliation they could wish on their enemies—to be eaten by dogs and crows, to descend from the status of warriors and predators into prey.

So much, then, for the hours—and years—you may have devoted to fitness. The muscles that have been so carefully sculpted and toned stiffen when calcium from the dead body leaks into them, causing rigor mortis, and loosening only when decomposition sets in. The organs we nurtured with supplements and superfoods abandon their appointed functions. The brain we have tamed with mindfulness exercises goes awry within minutes after the heart stops beating. Soon after, reports a forensic anthropologist, "the brain liquefies very quickly. It just pours out the ears and bubbles out the mouth."[27] Everything devolves into a stinking pool or, what may sound even worse, a morsel in a rat's digestive system.

If this sounds offensive, let me remind you that we inhabit an entertainment culture that is thickly populated with the "undead," the "walking dead," and other borderline creatures that resemble decaying corpses. Their mouths, always open to expose rotting teeth, are bloody gashes, their eyes are set deep in their sockets, their jowls may be beginning to melt down toward their necks, and of course, they are lurching toward us in search of a meal. This obsession is odd, given how meticulous our society is about the disposal of corpses. We are unlikely to trip over dead bodies on the sidewalk, but it is hard not to encounter them while relaxing in front of movies—as if we needed reminders of the postmortem future of the flesh.

CHAPTER ELEVEN

The Invention of the Self

We return now to a question raised earlier in this book. Who is in charge? We seek control over our bodies, our minds, and our lives, but who or what will be doing the controlling? The body can be ruled out because of its tendency to liquefy—or turn into dust—without artful embalming. So the entity we wish to enthrone must be invisible and perhaps immaterial—the mind, the spirit, the self, or perhaps some ineffable amalgam, as suggested by the phrase "mind, body, spirit" or the neologism "mindbody."

The spectacle of decomposition provides a powerful incentive to posit some sort of immaterial human essence that survives the body. Certainly there is very little talk of "mind-body unity" in the presence of a rotting corpse. In fact, the conversation is likely to take a different turn, to an emphasis on the existence of an immortal essence, or soul, that somehow carries on without the body. Medieval Catholic artists and clerics deployed images of decomposing bodies—sometimes with maggots wiggling in the nostrils and eye sockets—to underscore the urgency of preparing the soul for the disembodied life that awaits it. Buddhist monks practice "corpse meditation" in the presence of corpses, both fresh and rotting, to impress on themselves the impermanence of life. The soul, in both Christian and Islamic philosophy, is the perfect vessel for the immortality that eludes us as fleshly creatures: It's immortal by virtue of the fact it somehow participates in, or overlaps with, an immortal deity. Even nonbelievers today are likely to comfort themselves with the thought of a "soul," or spirit, or vague "legacy" that renders them impervious to decay. As Longfellow famously wrote, "Dust thou art, to dust returnest, was not spoken of the soul."[1]

But no one has detected this entity. There is in fact much firmer evidence for the existence of "dark matter," the hypothesized substance that is invoked to explain the shape of galaxies, than there is for any spirit or soul. At least dark matter can be detected indirectly through its gravitational effects. We can talk about someone's soul and whether it is capacious or shriveled, but we realize that we are speaking metaphorically. Various locations for an immaterial individual essence have been proposed—the heart, the brain, and the liver—but autopsies yield no trace of it, leading some to speculate that it is delocalized like the Chinese qi. In 1901, an American physician reported that the human body loses three-quarters of an ounce, or twenty-one grams, at the moment of death, arguing that this meant the soul is a material substance. But his experiment could not be replicated, suggesting that the soul, if it exists, possesses neither location nor mass. One can't even find the concept of the "immortal soul" in the Bible. It was grafted onto Christian teachings from the pagan Greeks long after the Bible was written.[2]

The idea of an immortal soul did not survive the Enlightenment unscathed. The soul depended on God to provide its immortality, and as his existence—or at least his attentiveness—was called into question, the immortal soul gave way to the far more secular notion of the self. While the soul was probably "discovered" by Christians (and Jews) reading Plato, the self was never discovered; it simply grew by accretion, apparently starting in Renaissance Europe. Scholars can argue endlessly about when exactly the idea of the self—or any other historical innovation—arose; precedents can always be claimed. But historians have generally agreed on the vague proposition that nothing like either the soul or the self existed in the ancient world. Ego, yes, and pride and ambition, but not the capacity for introspection and internal questioning that we associate with the self. Achilles wanted his name and his deeds remembered forever; he did not agonize over his motives or conflicted allegiances. That sort of thinking came later.

Lionel Trilling wrote that "in the late 16th and early 17th centuries, something like a mutation in human nature took place," which he took to be the requirement for what historian Frances Yates called "the emergence of modern European and American man."[3] As awareness of the individual self took hold, the bourgeoisie bought mirrors, commissioned portraits, wrote autobiographies, and increasingly honored the mission of trying to "find" oneself among the buzz of thought engendered by a crowded urban social world. Today we take it for granted that inside the self we present to others, there lies another, truer self, but the idea was still fresh in the 1780s when Jean-Jacques Rousseau announced triumphantly:

> I am forming an undertaking which has no precedent, and the execution of which will have no imitator whatsoever. I wish to show my fellows a man in all the truth of nature; and this man will be myself.
>
> Myself alone. I feel my heart and I know men. I am not made like any of the ones I have seen; I dare to believe that I am not made like any that exist. If I am worth no more, at least I am different.[4]

Megalomania, or the proud claim of a rebellious political thinker? Contemporary thought has leaned toward the latter; after all, Rousseau was a major intellectual influence on the French Revolution, which, whatever its bloody outcome, was probably the first mass movement to demand both individual "Liberté" and "Fraternité," or solidarity within the collective. There is something bracing about Rousseau's assertion of his individual self, but the important thing to remember is that it *was* an assertion—no evidence was offered, not that it is easy to imagine what kind of evidence that might be. As historian John O. Lyons put it, the self was "invented."[5]

Another slippery abstraction was taking hold at around the same time as the self, and this was the notion of "society." Like the self, society is not something you can point to or measure, it is a concept that has to be taught or shared, a ghostly entity that arises from an aggregate of individual selves. In material terms, you can imagine a "super-being" composed of numerous subunits clumsily trying to coordinate their movements. It is no coincidence that the concept of society arose along with that of the self, if only because the newly self-centered individual seemed to be mostly concerned with the opinion of others: How do I fit in? How do I compare to them? What impression am I making? We do not look into mirrors, for example, to see our "true" selves, but to see what others are seeing, and what passes for inner reflection is often an agonizing assessment of how others are judging us.

A psychological "mutation" of this magnitude cries out for a historic explanation. Here, historians have generally invoked the social and economic changes accompanying the increasing dominance of a market economy. As fixed feudal roles and obligations lost their grip, it became easier for people to imagine themselves as individuals capable of self-initiated change, including upward mobility. You might be an artisan and learn to dress and speak like a merchant, or a merchant who takes on the airs of an aristocrat. Traditional bonds of community and faith loosened, even making it possible to assume the identity of another person, as in the famous case of the sixteenth-century adventurer who managed to convince the inhabitants of a village that he was their missing neighbor Martin Guerre. He took over the family inheritance and moved in with the real Guerre's wife, at least until the ruse was uncovered three years later.[6] If you could move from village to village, from village to city, from one social class to another—and surely the disruptions of intra-European wars played a part in the new mobility—you have to constantly monitor the impression you are making on others. At the same time, those others are becoming less trustworthy; you cannot be sure what true "self" lies behind the façade.

Related to the rise of capitalism—though how related has long been a subject of debate—was the religious innovation represented by Protestantism, which midwifed the soul's transformation into the modern notion of the self. Pre-Reformation Catholics could ensure a blissful postmortem existence by participating in the sacraments or donating large sums to the church, but Protestants and especially Calvinists were assigned to perpetual introspection in an attempt to make their souls acceptable to God. Every transient thought and inclination had to be monitored for the slightest sinful impulse. As science and secularism chipped away at the notion of God, the habit of introspection remained. Psychoanalyst Garth Amundson writes:

> People continued to look inward, into the private life of the mind, so as to locate essential truths about their lives, though without the additional notion that these truths are the fruit of a dialogue with God's presence within the self. Hence, the Deity that Augustine thought that we discover by looking within the self was dethroned, and replaced by an invigorating confrontation with powerful private emotional states, fantasies, hopes, and needs. An authentic and immediate awareness of one's affective experience became the new center around which to create a life lived truthfully and "fully." In this way, the development of the private life of the self became something of an object of worship.[7]

Or, as somewhat more simply put by a Spanish historian, "the modern Rousseauist self, which feels and creates its own existence, would appear to be the heir to attributes previously assigned to God."[8]

In our own time, the language of self-regard has taken on a definite religious quality. We are instructed to "believe" in ourselves, "esteem" ourselves, be true to ourselves, and, above all, "love" ourselves, because otherwise how could anyone else love us? The endless cornucopia of "self-help" advice that began to overflow in the twentieth century enjoins us to be our own "best friends," to indulge ourselves, make time for ourselves, and often "celebrate" ourselves. If words like "believe" do not sufficiently suggest a religious stance, one site even urges us to "worship ourselves" by creating a shrine to oneself, which might include photos (probably "selfies"), favorite items of jewelry, and "nice smelling things such as perfume, candles or incense."[9] The self may seem like a patently false deity to worship, but it is no more—and no less—false than the God enshrined in recognized religions. Neither the self nor God is demonstrably present to everyone. Both require the exertion of "belief."

In today's capitalist culture the self has been further objectified into a kind of commodity demanding continual effort to maintain—a "brand." Celebrities clearly have well-defined "brands," composed of their talents, if any, their "personalities," and their physical images, all of which can be monetized and sold. Even lowly aspirants toward wealth and fame are encouraged to develop a brand and project it confidently into the world, and never mind if it is indistinguishable from that of millions of other people—cheerful, upbeat, and "positive-thinking" has been a favorite since the 1950s, both for office workers and CEOs. If some darker self, containing fears, resentments, and doubts, remains under your carefully constructed exterior, it is up to you to keep it under wraps. Internal "affirmations"—"I am confident, I am lovable, and I will be successful"—are thought to do the trick.

What could go wrong? Of course, with the introduction of "self-knowledge" and "self-love," one enters an endless hall of mirrors: How can the self be known to the self, and who is doing the knowing? If we love ourselves, who is doing the loving? This is the inescapable paradox of self-reflection: How can the self be both the knower and the content of what is known, both the subject and the object, the lover and that which is loved? Other people can be annoying, as Sartre famously suggested, but true hell is perpetual imprisonment in the self. Many historians have argued that the rise of self-awareness starting in roughly the seventeenth century was associated with the outbreak of an epidemic of "melancholy" in Europe at about the same time, and subjective accounts of that disorder correspond very closely with what we now call "depression."[10] Chronic anxiety, taking the form of "neurasthenia" in the nineteenth century, seems to be another disease of modernism. The self that we love and nurture turns out to be a fragile, untrustworthy thing.

Unlike the "soul" that preceded it, the self is mortal. When we are advised to "come to terms with" our mortality, we are not only meant to ponder our decaying corpses, but the almost unthinkable prospect of a world *without us in it*, or more precisely, a world without *me* in it, since I can, unfortunately, imagine a world without other people, even those I love most. A world without me, without a conscious "subject" to behold it, seems inherently paradoxical. As philosopher Herbert Fingarette writes:

> Could I imagine this familiar world continuing in existence even though I no longer exist? If I tried, it would be a world *imagined by me....* Yes, I can imagine a world without me in it as an inhabitant. But I can't imagine a world as unimagined by me. My consciousness of that world is ineliminable, and so, too, therefore, is my reaction to it. But this falsifies the meaning of my death, since its distinctive feature is that there won't be consciousness of, or reaction to, anything whatsoever.[11]

We are, most of the time, so deeply invested in the idea of an individual conscious self that it becomes both logically and emotionally impossible to think of a world without it. A physician who had narrowly escaped death more than once writes:

> Whenever I've tried wrapping my mind around the concept of my own demise—truly envisioned the world continuing on without me, the essence of what I am utterly gone forever—I've unearthed a fear so overwhelming my mind has been turned aside as if my imagination and the idea of my own end were two magnets of identical polarity, unwilling to meet no matter how hard I tried to make them.[12]

We may all imagine that some trace of ourselves will persist in the form of children and others whom we have influenced, or through the artifacts and intellectual products we leave behind. At the same time I know, though, that the particular constellation of memories, fantasies, and ambitions that is, for example, me will be gone. The unique—or so I like to imagine—thrum of my consciousness will be silenced, never to sound again. "All too often," wrote philosopher Robert C. Solomon, "we approach death with the self-indulgent thought that my death is a bad thing because it *deprives the universe of me*" (italics in the original).[13] Yet if we think about it, the universe survives the deaths of about fifty-five million unique individuals a year quite nicely.

In the face of death, secular people often scramble to expand their experiences or memorialize themselves in some lasting form. They may work their way through a "bucket list" of adventures and destinations or struggle to complete a cherished project. Or if they are at all rich or famous, they may dedicate their final years and months to the creation of a "legacy," such as a charitable foundation, in the same spirit as an emperor might plan his mausoleum. One well-known public figure of my acquaintance devoted some of his last months to planning a celebration of his life featuring adulatory speeches by numerous dignitaries including himself. Sadly, a couple of decades later, his name requires some explanation.

So the self becomes an obstacle to what we might call, in the fullest sense, "successful aging." I have seen accomplished people consumed in their final years with jockeying for one last promotion or other mark of recognition, or crankily defending their reputation against critics and potential critics. This is all that we in the modern world have learned how to do. And when we acquire painful neuroses from our efforts to promote and protect ourselves, we often turn to forms of therapy that require us to burrow even more deeply into ourselves. As Amundson writes, "the psychotherapy patient looks within for the truth, and comes away, not with anything that is considered universally valid or absolute in a metaphysical sense, but with a heightened and intensified devotion to such individualistic creeds as 'being true to oneself,' 'loving oneself,' and 'practicing self-care.'"[14]

There is one time-honored salve for the anxiety of approaching self-dissolution, and that is to submerge oneself into something "larger than oneself," some imagined super-being that will live on without us. The religious martyr dies for God, the soldier for the nation or, if his mind cannot encompass something as large as the nation, at least for the regiment or platoon. War is one of the oldest and most widespread human activities, and warriors are expected to face death willingly in battle, hoping to be memorialized in epics like the *Iliad* or the *Mahabharata* or in one of the war monuments that have sprung up since the nineteenth century. For frightened soldiers or, later, their grieving survivors, dying is reconfigured as a "sacrifice"—the "ultimate sacrifice"—with all the ancient religious connotations of an offering to the gods. And in case thoughts of eventual glory are not enough to banish fear, the US military is increasingly adopting the tools of alternative medicine, including meditation, dietary supplements, and reiki.[15] The expectation, though, is that true soldiers die calmly and without regret. As Winston Churchill said of poet and World War I recruit Rupert Brooke:

> He expected to die: he was willing to die for the dear England whose beauty and majesty he knew: and he advanced towards the brink in perfect serenity, with absolute conviction of the rightness of his country's cause and a heart devoid of hate for fellow-men.[16]

But you don't have to be a warrior to face death with equanimity. Anyone who lives for a cause like "the revolution" is entitled to imagine that cause being carried on by fresh generations, so that one's own death becomes a temporary interruption in a great chain of endeavor. Some stumble and fall or simply age out, but others will come along to carry on the work. As an old labor song about Joe Hill, a labor activist who was framed for murder and executed in 1915, tells us, it's as if death never happened at all:

> *I dreamed I saw Joe Hill last night*
> *Alive as you or me*
> *Says I, But Joe, you're ten years dead*
> *I never died, says he*
> *I never died, says he…*
>
> *Where working men are out on strike*
> *…Joe Hill is at their side*
> *Joe Hill is at their side*

From San Diego up to Maine
In every mine and mill
Where workers strike and organize
Says he, You'll find Joe Hill[17]

The revolutionary lives and dies for her people, secure in her belief that someone else will pick up the banner when she falls. To the true believer, individual death is incidental. *A luta continua.*

The idea of a super-being that will outlive us as individuals is not entirely delusional. Human beings are among the most sociable of living creatures. Studies of orphaned infants in World War II showed that even if kept warm and adequately fed, infants who were not held and touched "failed to thrive" and eventually died.[18] Socially isolated adults are less likely to survive trauma and disease than those embedded in family and community. We delight in occasions for unified, collective expression, whether in the form of dancing, singing, or chanting for a demagogue. Even our most private thoughts are shaped by the structure of language, which is of course also our usual medium of interaction with others. And as many have argued, we are ever more tightly entangled by the Internet into a single global mind—although in a culture as self-centric as ours, the Internet can also be used as a mirror, or a way to rate ourselves by the amount of attention we are getting from others, the number of "likes."

It is the idea of a continuous chain of human experience and endeavor that has kept me going through an unexpectedly long life. I will stumble and fall; in fact, I already stumble a lot, but others will pick up the torch and continue the race. It's not only "my work"—forgive the pompous phrase—that I bequeath to my survivors but all the mental and sensual pleasures that come with being a living human: sitting in the spring sunshine, feeling the warmth of friends, solving a difficult equation. All that will go on without me. I am content, in the time that remains, to be a transient cell in the larger human super-being.

But there are flaws in this philosophic perspective. For one thing, it is entirely anthropocentric. Why shouldn't our "great chain of being" include the other creatures with which we have shared the planet, the creatures we have martyred in service to us or driven out of their homes to make way for our expansion? Surely we have some emotional attachment to them, even if it is hard to imagine passing the figurative torch to dogs or, in one of the worst scenarios, insects and microbes.

Then there is a deeper, more existential problem with my effort to derive some comfort from the notion of an ongoing human super-being: Our species itself appears to be mortal and, in many accounts, imminently doomed, most likely to die by our own hand, through global warming or nuclear war. Some scientists put the chance of a "near extinction event," in which up to 10 percent of our species is wiped out, at a little over 9 percent within a hundred years.[19] Others doubt our species will survive the current century. As environmentalist Daniel Drumright writes—and I can only hope he is an alarmist—with the growing awareness of extinction, "We're dealing with a discovery of such epic proportion that it simply reduces everything in existence to nothing." He goes on to say that our emerging circumstances require "a diabolic consciousness to which no living human being has ever had to bear witness. It is an awareness which requires a degree of emotional maturity that's almost indistinguishable from insanity within western culture."[20]

If your imagination is vigorous enough, you may take comfort from the likely existence of other forms of life throughout the universe. Earth-sized planets abound, potentially offering other habitats similar to our own, with reasonable temperatures and abundant water. In addition, sci-fi fans know that our vision of life based on carbon and water is likely to be far too provincial. There may be life forms based on other chemicals, or self-reproducing entities that do not even consist of conventional matter—patterns of energy bursts, oscillating currents, gluttonous black holes; already we have artificial life in the form of computer programs that can reproduce and evolve to meet changing circumstances. And—who knows?—some of these "life" forms may be suitable heirs for our species, capable of questing and loving.

But even here our yearning for immortality runs into a wall, because the universe itself will come to an end if current predictions are borne out, whether in 2.8 or 22 billion years from now, which of course still gives us plenty of time to get our things in order. In one scenario there will be a "big crunch" in which expansionist forces will rip even atoms apart. In another, the night sky will empty out, the huge void spaces now separating galaxies will grow until they swallow everything. Vacuum and perfect darkness will prevail. Both scenarios lead to the ultimate nightmare of a world "without us in it," and it is infinitely bleaker than a world without our individual selves—a world, if you can call it that, without anything in it, not the tiniest spark of consciousness or wisp of energy or matter. To cruelly paraphrase Martin Luther King, the arc of history is long, but it bends toward catastrophic annihilation.

CHAPTER TWELVE

Killing the Self, Rejoicing in a Living World

Philosophically, we have painted ourselves into a corner. On the one hand, we posit a lifeless material world. As the twentieth-century biochemist Jacques Monod put it, in what I can only imagine was a tone of bitter triumph, "Man at last knows he is alone in the unfeeling immensity of the universe."[1] On the other hand, we hold on to the perception of an endlessly fascinating self, bloated now by at least a century of self-love and self-absorption. We live like fugitives, always trying to keep one step ahead of the inevitable annihilation—one more meal, one more dollar or fortune to win, one more workout or medical screening. And we die…Well, we cannot die at all because the death of the self is unthinkable.

The traditional solution to this existential dilemma has been to simply *assert* the existence of a conscious agency other than ourselves, in the form of a deity, an assertion that has often been backed up by coercion. For about two thousand years, large numbers of people—today a clear majority of the world's population[2]—have either insisted that this deity is a single all-powerful individual, or they have at least pretended to go along with the idea. Perhaps to make this remote and solitary god more palatable, the "world religions" also assert that he is all-good and all-loving, although this bit of PR had the effect of making him seem preposterous, since a good and loving god would not unleash earthquakes or kill babies. Belief in such a deity takes considerable effort, as many Europeans discovered after the eighteenth-century earthquake that destroyed Lisbon. But it is an effort that most people are willing to make since the alternative is so ghastly: How can anyone live knowing that they will end up as a pile of refuse? Or, as atheists are often asked, how can we die knowing death is followed only by nothingness?

The rise of monotheism has been almost universally hailed by modern scholars as a great moral and intellectual step forward. In myth, the transition to monotheism sometimes occurred as a usurpation of divine power by a particular polytheistic deity within a larger pantheon: Yahweh, for example, had to drive out the earlier Canaanite gods like Asherah and Baal. Politically, the transition could occur suddenly by kingly decree, as in the cases of the pharaoh Akhenaten, the Hebrew king Saul, and the emperor Constantine. The single God's exclusive claim to represent perfect goodness (or, in the case of Yahweh, fierce tribal loyalty) proved, in turn, crucial in legitimating the power of the king, who could claim to rule by divine right. The system is ethically tidy: All morally vexing questions can be answered with the claim that the one deity is the perfection of goodness, even if his motives are inscrutable to us.

But the transition to monotheism can also be seen as a long process of deicide, a relentless culling of the ancient gods and spirits until no one was left except an abstraction so distant that it required "belief." The "primitive"—and perhaps original—human picture was of a natural world crowded with living spirits: animals that spoke and understood human languages, mountains and rivers that encapsulated autonomous beings and required human respect and attention. The nineteenth-century anthropologist Edward Tylor termed this view of an inspirited world "animism," and to this day, indigenous belief systems that seem particularly disorganized and incoherent compared to the great "world religions" like Islam and Christianity are also labeled—or perhaps we should say libeled—as animism.

Historically, animism was followed by polytheism. How the multitudinous spirits of animism congealed into distinct deities is not known, but the earliest polytheistic religion is thought to be Hinduism, arising in about 2500 BCE and still bearing traces of animism in the form of animal deities like Ganesh and Hanuman, as well as in rural shrines centered on rocks. The religions of the ancient Mediterranean world, the Middle East, and the southern part of the Western Hemisphere were all polytheistic, made possible by stratified societies capable of erecting temples and supporting a nonproductive priestly caste.

Not everyone went along cheerfully with the imposition of monotheism, which required the abandonment of so many familiar deities, animal gods, and spirits, along with their attendant festivities. The Egyptians reverted to polytheism as soon as Akhenaten died, while the Hebrew kings fought ruthlessly to suppress their subjects' constant backsliding to the old Canaanite religion. Within the monotheistic religions too, there was a steady drift back toward polytheism. The Christian God divided himself into the Trinity; saints proliferated within Christianity and Islam; the remnants of animism flourish alongside Buddhism (which, strictly speaking, shouldn't be considered a form of theism at all).

In the last five hundred years "reform" movements rushed in to curb these deviations. In Europe the Reformation cracked down on the veneration of saints, downplayed the Trinity, and stripped churches of decoration, incense, and other special effects. Within Islam, Wahhabism suppressed Sufism, along with music and artistic depictions of living creatures. The face of religion became blank and featureless, as if to discourage the mere imagining of non-human agencies in the world.

It was the austere, reformed version of monotheism that set the stage for the rise of modern reductionist science, which took as its mission the elimination of agency from the natural world. Science did not set out to destroy the monotheistic deity; in fact, as Jessica Riskin explains, it initially gave him a lot more work to do. If nature is devoid of agency, then everything depends on a "Prime Mover" to breathe life into the world.[3] But science pushed him into a corner and ultimately rendered him irrelevant. When an iconic 1966 *Time* magazine cover echoed Nietzsche by asking, "Is God Dead?" the word was out: We humans are alone in a dead universe, the last conscious beings left. This was the intellectual backdrop for the deification of the "self."

It is too late to revive the deities and spirits that enlivened the world of our ancestors, and efforts to do so are invariably fatuous. But we can begin to loosen the skeletal grip of the old, necrophiliac science on our minds. In fact, for the sake of scientific rationality, we have to. As Jackson Lears has written recently, the reductionist science that condemns the natural world to death "is not 'science' per se but a singular, historically contingent version of it—a version that depends on the notion that nature is a passive mechanism, the operations of which are observable, predictable, and subject to the law-like rules that govern inert matter."[4]

Only grudgingly, science has conceded agency to life at the cellular level, where researchers now admit that "decisions" are made about where to go and what other cells to kill or make alliances with. This gradual change of mind about agency at the microscopic level is analogous to the increasing scientific acceptance of emotion, reasoning, and even consciousness in nonhuman animals—which was belatedly acknowledged at an international conference of neuroscientists in 2012.[5] As for myself, I am not entirely satisfied with the notion of cellular decision making and would like to know more about how cells arrive at their decisions and how humans could perhaps intervene. But I no longer expect to find out that these decisions are "determined"—in the old Newtonian sense of, say, a rock falling in response to gravity, or by perhaps any forces or factors outside of the cell.

The question I started with has to do with human health and the possibility of our controlling it. If I had known that this is just part of a larger question about whether the natural world is dead or in some sense alive, I might have started in many other places, for example with fruit flies, viruses, or electrons that, according to the scientists who study them, appear to possess "free will" or the power to make "decisions." Wherever we look, if we look closely enough, we find nature defying the notion of a dead, inert universe. Science has tended to dismiss the innate activities of matter as Brownian motion or "stochastic noise"—the fuzziness that inevitably arises when we try to measure or observe something, which is in human terms little more than a nuisance. But some of these activities are far more consequential, and do not even require matter to incubate them. In a perfect void, pairs of particles and antiparticles can appear out of nowhere without violating any laws of physics. As Stephen Hawking puts it, "We are the product of quantum fluctuations in the very early universe. God really does play dice."[6] Most of these spontaneously generated particle pairs or "quantum fluctuations" are transient and flicker quickly out of existence. But every few billion years or so, a few occur simultaneously and glom together to form a building block of matter, perhaps leading, in a few billion more years, to a new universe.

Maybe then, our animist ancestors were on to something that we have lost sight of in the last few hundred years of rigid monotheism, science, and Enlightenment. And that is the insight that the natural world is not dead, but swarming with activity, sometimes perhaps even agency and intentionality. Even the place where you might expect to find quiet and solidity, the very heart of matter—the interior of a proton or a neutron—turns out to be animated with the ghostly flickerings of quantum fluctuations.[7] I would not say that the universe is "alive," since that might invite misleading biological analogies. But it is restless, quivering, and juddering, from its vast vacant patches to its tiniest crevices.

I have done my feeble best here to refute the idea of dead matter. But the other part of the way out of our dilemma is to confront the monstrous self that occludes our vision, separates us from other beings, and makes death such an intolerable prospect. Susan Sontag, who spent her last couple of years "battling" her cancer, as the common military metaphor goes, once wrote in her journal, "Death is unbearable unless you can get beyond the 'I.'"[8] In his book on her death, her son, David Rieff, commented, "But she who could do so many things in her life could never do that,"[9] and devoted her last years and months to an escalating series of medical tortures, each promising to add some extra months to her life.

Just a few years ago, I despaired of any critical discussion of the self as an obstacle to a peaceful death without getting mired in the slippery realm of psychoanalysis or the even more intimidating discourse of postmodern philosophy. But a surprising new line of scientific inquiry has opened up in an area long proscribed, and in fact criminalized—the study of psychedelic drugs. Reports of their use in treating depression, in particular the anxiety and depression of the terminally ill, started surfacing in the media about a decade ago. The intriguing point for our purposes here is that these drugs seem to act by suppressing or temporarily abolishing the sense of "self."

The new research has been masterfully summarized in a

2015 article by science writer Michael Pollan.[10] In a typical trial, the patient—usually someone suffering from cancer—receives a dose of psilocybin, the active ingredient in "magic mushrooms," lies on a couch in a soothingly appointed room, and "trips" for several hours under the watchful eye of a physician. When the drug wears off, the patient is asked to prepare a detailed chronicle of his or her experience and submit to frequent follow-up interviews. Pollan quotes one of the researchers, a New York University psychiatrist, on the preliminary results:

> People who had been palpably scared of death—they lost their fear. The fact that a drug given once can have such an effect for so long [up to six months] is an unprecedented finding. We have never had anything like it in the psychiatric field.[11]

When the subjective accounts of patients are supplemented with scans to localize brain activity, it turns out that the drug's effect is to suppress the part of the brain concerned with the sense of self, the "default-mode network." The more thoroughly this function of the brain is suppressed, the more the patient's reported experience resembles a spontaneously occurring mystical experience, in which a person goes through "ego dissolution" or the death of the self—which can be terrifying—followed by a profound sense of unity with the universe, with which the fear of death falls away. And the more intense the psychedelic trip or mystical experience, the more strikingly anxiety and depression are abolished in the patient. A fifty-four-year-old TV news director with terminal cancer reported during his medically supervised psilocybin trip, "Oh God, it all makes sense now, so simple and beautiful." He added later, "Even the germs were beautiful, as was everything in our world and universe."[12] He died, apparently contently, seventeen months later. This sense of an animate universe is confirmed by the subjective account of a psilocybin experience from a British psychologist who was otherwise well and not part of a laboratory study:

> At a certain point, you are shifted into an animate, supernormal reality....Beauty can radiate from everything that one sets one's eyes on, as though one had suddenly woken up more. Everything appears as if alive and in fluidic connection.[13]

In some ways, the ego or self is a great achievement. Certainly it is hard to imagine human history without this internal engine of conquest and discovery. The self keeps us vigilant and alert to threats; vanity helps drive some of our finest accomplishments. Especially in a highly competitive capitalist culture, how would anyone survive without a well-honed, highly responsive ego? But as Pollan observes:

> The sovereign ego can become a despot. This is perhaps most evident in depression, when the self turns on itself and uncontrollable introspection gradually shades out reality.[14]

The same sort of thing can be said of the immune system. It saves us time and again from marauding microbes, but it can also betray us with deadly effect. The philosopher/

immunologist Alfred Tauber wrote of the self as a metaphor for the immune system, but that metaphor can be turned around to say that the immune system is a metaphor for the self. Its ostensible job is the defense of the organism, but it is potentially a treacherous defender, like the Praetorian guard that turns its swords against the emperor. Just as the immune system can unleash the inflammations that ultimately kill us, the self can pick at a psychic scar—often some sense of defeat or abandonment—until a detectable illness appears, such as obsessive-compulsive disorder, depression, or crippling anxiety.

So what am I? Or, since individual personality is not the issue here, I might as well ask, what are you? First, the body: It is not a clumsy burden we drag around with us everywhere, nor is it an endlessly malleable lump of clay. Centuries of dissection and microscopy have revealed that it is composed of distinct organs, tissues, and cells, which are connected to form a sort of system—first conceived of as a machine, and more recently as a harmonious interlocking "whole." But the closer we look, the less harmonious and smooth-running the body becomes. It seethes with cellular life, sometimes even warring cells that appear to have no interest in the survival of the whole organism.

Then, the mind, the conscious mind, and here I am relying, appropriately I think, solely on subjective experience: We may imagine that the mind houses a singular self, an essence of "I-ness," distinct from all other selves and consistent over time. But attend closely to your thoughts and you find they are thoroughly colonized by the thoughts of others, through language, culture, and mutual expectations.

The answer to the question of what I am, or you are, requires some historical and geographical setting.

Nor is there at the core of mind some immutable kernel. The process of thinking involves conflict and alliances between different patterns of neuronal activity. Some patterns synchronize with and reinforce each other. Others tend to cancel each other, and not all of them contribute to our survival. Depression, for example, or anorexia or compulsive risk taking, represent patterns of synaptic firing that carve deep channels in the mind (and brain), not easily controlled by conscious effort, and sometimes lethal for the organism as a whole, both body and mind. So of course we die, even without help from natural disasters or plagues: We are gnawing away at ourselves all the time, whether with our overactive immune cells or suicidal patterns of thought.

I began this book at a point where death was no longer an entirely theoretical prospect. I had reached a chronological status that could not be euphemized as "middle-aged" and the resulting age-related limitations were becoming harder to deny. Three years later, I continue to elude unnecessary medical attention and still doggedly push myself in the gym, where, if I am no longer a star, I am at least a fixture. In addition, I retain a daily regimen of stretching, some of which might qualify as yoga. Other than that, I pretty much eat what I want and indulge my vices, from butter to wine. Life is too short to forgo these pleasures, and would be far too long without them.

Two years ago, I sat in a shady backyard around a table of friends, all over sixty, when the conversation turned to the age-appropriate subject of death. Most of those present averred that they were not afraid of death, only of any suffering that might be involved in dying. I did my best to assure them that this could be minimized or eliminated by insisting on a nonmedical death, without the torment of heroic interventions to prolong life by a few hours or days. Furthermore, we now potentially have the means to make the end of life more comfortable, if not actually pleasant— hospices, painkillers, and psychedelics, even, in some places, laws permitting assisted suicide. At least for those who are able to access these, there is little personal suffering to fear. Regret, certainly, and one of my most acute regrets is that I will not be around to monitor scientific progress in the areas that interest me, which is pretty much everything. Nor am I likely to witness what I suspect is the coming deep paradigm shift from a science based on the assumption of a dead universe to one that acknowledges and seeks to understand a natural world shot through with nonhuman agency.

It is one thing to die into a dead world and, metaphorically speaking, leave one's bones to bleach on a desert lit only by a dying star. It is another thing to die into the actual world, which seethes with life, with agency other than our own, and, at the very least, with endless possibility. For those of us, which is probably most of us, who—with or without drugs or religion—have caught glimpses of this animate universe, death is not a terrifying leap into the abyss, but more like an embrace of ongoing life. On his deathbed in 1956, Bertolt Brecht wrote one last poem:

When in my white room at the Charité
I woke towards morning

And heard the blackbird, I understood
Better. Already for some time
I had lost all fear of death. For nothing
Can be wrong with me if I myself
Am nothing. Now
I managed to enjoy
The song of every blackbird after me too.[15]

He was dying, but that was all right. The blackbirds would keep on singing.

ACKNOWLEDGMENTS

Not everyone I talked to about this project was enthusiastic. Some people found the subject too esoteric; specialists sometimes seemed to resent the intrusion of a mere writer into their fields. So I am intensely grateful to the people who did provide insights and encouragement along the way: my longtime friend sociologist Arlie Hochschild, anthropologist Erica Lagalisse, the various scholars who took time to talk to me, and my editors John Summers and Chris Lehman at *The Baffler,* where earlier versions of some bits of this book were published. Blame them for this book, since they unfailingly abetted my peculiar fascinations.

Chief among my enablers was my endlessly patient and intellectually supple agent, Kristine Dahl, as well as Deb Futter, the editor at Twelve who took the leap of offering me a contract. Deb's successor at Twelve, Sean Desmond, bludgeoned earlier drafts into some semblance of coherence and also did a great deal to enliven the end product. Thanks, Sean, and thanks also to the sharp-eyed copy editor Roland Ottewell.

For the first time as an author I felt I needed a fact-checker and had the dazzlingly good fortune of finding Yasha Hartberg (thanks here to evolutionary biologist David Sloan Wilson), who was as comfortable with the scientific literature as with philosophy, history, sociology, and popular culture.

In addition to all these energetically supportive people, I had the help of my own personal posse, starting with my children, Rosa Brooks and Ben Ehrenreich. Both of them published books of their own while I was working on this one but still found time to read and comment on my drafts. My former husband, John Ehrenreich, who also published a book during this period, along with his wife, Sharon McQuaide, managed to provide valuable comments on this one. I am especially grateful to my colleague Alissa Quart at the Economic Hardship Reporting Project—a superb writer and editor—whom I also enlisted.

As a long-overdue homage, this book is dedicated to my thesis adviser at Rockefeller University, the brilliant and kindly immunologist Zanvil A. Cohn, whom I grievously disappointed by going off to become a writer and activist. He died in 1993, before I had a chance to formally apologize for what must have seemed a gross misuse of his time. If he had lived longer, I like to imagine that he would have seen this book as a small step toward compensation.

ENDNOTES

INTRODUCTION

1. Gary Stix, "A Malignant Flame," *Scientific American*, July 1, 2008, www.scientificamerican.com/article/a-malignant-flame-2008-07/

CHAPTER ONE: MIDLIFE REVOLT

1. Alix Spiegel, "How a Bone Disease Grew to Fit the Prescription," *All Things Considered*, NPR, December 21, 2009, www.npr.org/2009/12/21/121609815/how-a-bone-disease-grew-to-fit-the-prescription.
2. Paula Span, "Too Many Colonoscopies in the Elderly," *The New Old Age* (blog), *New York Times*, March 12, 2013, http://newoldage.blogs.nytimes.com/2013/03/12/too-many-colonoscopies-in-the-elderly/?_r=1&module=ArrowsNav &contentCollection=Health&action=keypress&region=FixedLeft&pgtype=Blogs.
3. John M. Mandrola, "Redefining the Annual Physical: A (Broken) Window into American Healthcare," Medscape, January 15, 2015, www.medscape.com/viewarticle/838132.
4. Sandra G. Boodman, "Seniors Get More Medical Tests Than Are Good for Them, Experts Say," *Washington Post*, September 12, 2011, www.washingtonpost.com/national/health-science/seniors-get-more-medical-tests-than-are-good-for-them-experts-say/2011/

08/10/gIQAX3OWNK_story.html?utm_term= .4eff254f9fcc.

5. Ibid.

6. "The PSA Test: What's Right for You?," *Harvard Men's Health Watch*, March 2012, www.health.harvard.edu/mens-health/the-psa-test-whats-right-for-you.

7. Gina Kolata, "Got a Thyroid Tumor? Most Should Be Left Alone," *New York Times*, August 22, 2016, www.nytimes.com/2016/08/23/health/got-a-thyroid-tumor-most-should-be-left-alone.html?_r=0.

8. John Horgan, "Why I Won't Get a Colonoscopy," *Cross-Check* (blog), *Scientific American*, March 12, 2012, https://blogs.scientificamerican.com/cross-check/why-i-wont-get-a-colonoscopy/.

9. Ken Murray, "Why Doctors Die Differently," *Wall Street Journal*, February 25, 2012, www.wsj.com/articles/SB10001424052970203918304577243321242833962.

CHAPTER TWO: RITUALS OF HUMILIATION

1. Oxford Living Dictionaries, "ritual" (definition), https://en.oxforddictionaries.com/defi nition/ritual.

2. Edith Turner, *Experiencing Ritual: A New Interpretation of African Healing* (Philadelphia: University of Pennsylvania Press, 2011).

3. Simon Sinclair, "Evidence-Based Medicine: A New Ritual in Medical Teaching," *British Medical Bulletin* 69, no. 1 (June 2004): 179–96, http://bmb.oxfordjournals.org/content/69/1/179.full.

4. Horace Miner, "Body Rituals Among the Nacirema," *American Anthropologist* 58, no. 3 (June 1956): 503–7, available at https://msu.edu/~jdowell/miner.html.

5. Adam Burtle, "Doctors, Shamans, and Clowns," *Structural Violence*, May 3, 2013, www.structuralviolence.org/1273/doctors-shamans-and-clowns/.

6. Anne Fox, "Drink and Duty: Extreme Drinking Rituals in the British Army," in *The Character of Human Institutions*, ed. Michael Egan (New Brunswick, NJ: Transaction, 2014), 74.

7. Ellen Frankfort, personal communication.

8. Robbie E. Davis-Floyd, *Birth as an American Rite of Passage* (Berkeley: University of California Press, 2003), 115.

9. Quoted in ibid., 87.

10. Quoted in ibid., 127.

11. Ivan Illich, *Medical Nemesis: The Expropriation of Health* (New York: Pantheon, 1976), chapter 2, "The Medicalization of Life," available at http://soilandhealth.org/wp-content/uploads/0303-critic/030313illich/Frame.Illich.Ch2.html.

12. Irving Kenneth Zola, "Structural Constraints in the Doctor-Patient Relationship: The Case of Non-Compli ance," in *The Relevance of Social Science for Medicine*, ed. Leon Eisenberg and Arthur Kleinman (Boston: D. Reidel Publishing Company, 1981), 245.

13. Abraham Verghese, "Treat the Patient, Not the CT Scan" (op-ed), *New York Times*, February 26, 2011, www.nytimes.com/2011/02/27/opin ion/27verghese.html.

14. Abraham Verghese, "A Doctor's Touch," TED talk, July 2011, www.ted.com/talks/abraham_ verghese_a_doctor_s_touch/transcript?language=en.

15. Ibid.

16. Cara Feinberg, "The Placebo Phenomenon," *Harvard* magazine, January–February 2013, http://harvardmagazine.com/2013/01/the-placebo-phenomenon.

17. David Cameron, "Placebos Work—Even Without Deception," *Harvard Gazette*, December 22, 2010, http://news.harvard.edu/gazette/story/2010/12/placebos-work-%E2%80%94-even-without-deception/.

CHAPTER THREE: THE VENEER OF SCIENCE

1. Craig Lambert, "The New Ancient Trend in Medicine," *Harvard* magazine, March–April 2002, http://harvardmagazine.com/2002/03/the-new-ancient-trend-in-html.

2. David M. Eddy, "The Origins of Evidence-Based Medicine—A Personal Perspective," *Virtual Mentor* 13, no. 1 (2011): 55–60, http://journalofethics.ama-assn.org/2011/01/mhst1-1101.html.

3. Ibid.

4. Gary Schwitzer, "Roundup of Some Reactions to NEJM Mammography Overdiagnosis Analysis," *Health News Review*, November 23, 2012, www.healthnewsreview.org/2012/11/roundup-of-some-reactions-to-nejm-mammography-overdiagnosis-analysis/.

5.   "Do Biopsies Spread Cancer?," *PR Newswire*, August 23, 2012, www.prnewswire.com/news-releases/ do-biopsies-spread-cancer-167177565.html.

6.   National Cancer Institute, "Long-Term Trial Results Show No Mortality Benefit from Annual Prostate Cancer Screening," February 17, 2012, www.cancer.gov/clinicaltrials/results/summary/2012/PLCO-prostate-screening0112.

7.   Otis Brawley, "Epidemic of Overtreatment of Prostate Cancer Must Stop," CNN, July 18, 2014, www.cnn.com/2014/07/18/health/prostate-cancer-overtreament/.

8.   Andrew Pollack, "Looser Guidelines Issued on Prostate Screening," *New York Times*, May 3, 2013, www.nytimes.com/2013/05/04/ business/prostate-screening-guidelines-are-loosened.html.

9.   Elisabeth Rosenthal, "The $2.7 Trillion Medical Bill," *New York Times*, June 1, 2013, www.nytimes.com/2013/06/02/health/colonoscopies-explain-why-us-leads-the-world-in-health-expenditures.html?pagewanted=all&_r=0.

10. Stephanie O'Neill, "Too Many Are Getting Unnecessary Prostate Treatment, UCLA Study Says," SCPR 89.3 KPCC, December 21, 2014, www.scpr.org/news/2014/12/01/48398/too-many-are-getting-unnecessary-prostate-treatmen/.

11. http://108.163.177.220/print_frame.php?action=chapter&node=57639.

12. Jenny Gold, "Your Annual Physical Is a Costly Ritual, Not Smart Medicine," CNN, April 14, 2015, www.cnn.com/2015/04/14/health/annual-physical-ritual-costly/.

13. Audio clip from *Mad Men* at Hark.com, www.hark.com/clips/dhvqltmpww-dont-think-you-have-to-go-out-and-become-the-town-pump.

14. Kathryn Joyce, "The Silence of the Lambs," *New Republic*, July 2017, 39.

15. "Psychological Harms of Pelvic Exams," *For Women's Eyes Only*, January 2, 2013, http://forwomenseyesonly.com/2013/01/02/psychological-harms-of-pelvic-exams/.

16. Lenny Bernstein, "Healthy Women Do Not Need Routine Pelvic Exams, Influential Physicians Group Says," *Washington Post*, June 30, 2014, www.washingtonpost.com/news/to-your-health/wp/2014/06/30/healthy-women-do-not-need-routine-pelvic-exams-influential-physicians-group-says/.

17. Gina Kolata, "Annual Physical Checkup May Be an Empty Ritual," *New York Times*, August 12, 2003.

18. Peter Cappelli, "The Return of the Executive Physical," Human Resource Executive Online, March 5, 2007, www.hreonline.com/ HRE/view/story.jhtml?id=10026321.

19. Anthony L. Komaroff, "Executive Physicals: What's the ROI?," *Harvard Business Review*, September 2009, https://hbr.org/2009/ 09/executive-physicals-whats-the-roi.

20. Arthur L. Caplan, "No Method, Thus Madness?," Center for Bioethics Papers, University of Pennsylvania Scholarly Commons, http://repository.upenn.edu/cgi/viewcontent. cgi?article=1042&context=bioethics _papers.

21. Ibid.

22. Quoted in Angus Rae, "Osler Vindicated: The Ghost of Flexner Laid to Rest," *Canadian Medical Association Journal* 164, no. 13 (2001): 1860–61, www.ncbi.nlm.nih.gov/pmc/articles/ PMC81198/#r3-18.

23. Quoted in Robbie E. Davis-Floyd, *Birth as an American Rite of Passage* (Berkeley: University of California Press, 2003), 256.

24. Abraham Flexner, *Medical Education in the United States and Canada: A Report to the Carnegie Foundation for the Advancement of Teaching* (Boston: D. B. Updike, The Merrymount Press, 1910), 18.

25. Robb Burlage, personal communication.

26. Melvin Konner, *Becoming a Doctor: A Journey of Initiation in Medical School* (New York: Penguin, 1987), 38.

27. Jeffrey P. Bishop, *The Anticipatory Corpse: Medicine, Power, and the Care of the Dying* (Notre Dame, IN: Notre Dame University Press, 2011).

28. Ibid.

29. Farr A. Curlin, "Detachment Has Consequences: A Note of Caution from Medical Students' Experiences of Cadaver Dissection," in John D. Lantos, ed., *Controversial Bodies: Thoughts on the Public Display of Plastinated Corpses* (Baltimore: Johns Hopkins University Press, 2011), 57.

30. Konner, *Becoming a Doctor*, 373.

31. Ibid.

32. Kolata, "Annual Physical Checkup May Be an Empty Ritual."

33. Alice W. Flaherty, "Performing the Art of Medicine," *Total Art*, http://totalartjournal.com/archives/1186/performing-the-art-of-medicine/.

34. "How Doctors Think," *Fresh Air*, NPR, March 14, 2007, www.npr.org/templates/story/story.php?storyId=8892053.

CHAPTER FOUR: CRUSHING THE BODY

1. International Health, Racquet & Sportsclub Association, "Global Fitness Industry Records Another Year of Growth," May 25, 2016, www.ihrsa.org/news/2016/5/25/global-fitness-industry-records-another-year-of-growth.html.

2. Quoted in Marc Stern, "The Fitness Movement and the Fitness Center Industry, 1960–2000," *Business and Economic History On-Line* 6 (2008): 5, www.thebhc.org/sites/default/files/stern_0.pdf.

3. Quoted in Herb Hennings, "Over the Hill" (column), *Kenyon Collegian*, December 4, 1969, http://digital.kenyon.edu/cgi/view-con tent.cgi?article=3312&context =collegian.

4. "Why So Many Ph.D.s Are on Food Stamps," *Tell Me More*, NPR, May 15, 2012, www.npr.org/2012/05/15/152751116/why-so-many-ph-d-s-are-on-food-stamps.

5. "More College Freshmen Plan to Teach: A Decrease in Altruism and Social Concern Is Found," *New York Times*, January 12, 1987, A15.

6. Quoted in Stern, "The Fitness Movement and the Fitness Center Industry," 6.

7. James Fixx, *The Complete Book of Running* (New York: Random House, 1977), 14.

8. Gloria Steinem, "The Politics of Muscle," available at http://eng101fall09.wikispaces.com/file/view/Steinem_The+Politics+of+Muscle.pdf.

9. Sharon Tanenbaum, "Jane Fonda Opens Up About Her Decades-Long Battle with Bulimia," *Everyday Health*, August 9, 2011, www.everydayhealth.com/eating-disor ders/0809/jane-fonda-opens-up-about-her-decades-long-battle-with-bulimia.aspx.

10. "The Soft Science of Dietary Fat," *Science* 291 (March 30, 2001): 2536–45, http://garytaubes.com/wp-content/uploads/2011/08/Science-The-soft-science-of-dietary-fat-21.pdf.

11. Wanda Urbanska, *The Singular Generation: Young Americans in the 1980's* (New York: Doubleday, 1986), 100–101.

12. Delmore Schwartz, "The Heavy Bear," quoted in Susan Bordo, *Unbearable Weight: Feminism, Western Culture, and the Body*, 10th anniversary ed. (Berkeley: University of California Press, 2003), 1.

13. Allison Van Dusen, "Is Your Weight Affecting Your Career?," *Forbes*, May 21, 2008, www.forbes.com/2008/05/21/health-weight-career-forbeslife-cx_avd_0521health.html.

14. Leah Binder, "Three Surprising Hazards of Worksite Wellness Pro-

grams," *Forbes*, February 4, 2014, www.forbes.com/sites/leah-binder/2014/02/04/three-surprising-hazards-of-worksite-wellness-programs/#51e20027466a.

15. Rand Corporation, "Do Workplace Wellness Programs Save Employers Money?," www.rand.org/pubs/ research_briefs/RB9744.html.

16. John H. Knowles, ed., *Doing Better and Feeling Worse* (New York: W. W. Norton, 1977), 59.

17. Quoted in Howard M. Leichter, "'Evil Habits' and 'Personal Choices': Assigning Responsibility for Health in the 20th Century," *Milbank Quarterly* 81, no. 4 (December 2003): 603–26, www.ncbi.nlm.nih.gov/pmc/articles/PMC2690243/.

18. Bipartisan Policy Center, "Are America's Physicians Prepared to Combat the Obesity Epidemic?," June 23, 2014, http://bipartisanpolicy.org/library/are-americas-physicians-prepared-to-combat-the-obesity-epidemic/.

19. Paula Cohen, "Group of Doctors Calls on Columbia Univ. to Oust Dr. Oz," CBS News, April 16, 2015, www.cbsnews.com/news/group-of-doctors-call-for-dr-oz-to-be-ousted-from-columbia-university/.

20. "The Yuppie America's Economic Savior…Former Anti-war Activist Jerry Rubin Now Preaches the Gospel of Yuppiedom, Claiming That Yuppies Are Responsible for America's Current Good Economy," SunSentinel.com, October 19, 1985, http://articles.sun-sentinel.com/1985-10-19/features/8502150535_1_yuppies-new-movement-real-estate.

21. Josh Bersin, "Quantified Self: Meet the Quantified Employee," *Forbes*, June 25, 2014, www.forbes.com/sites/joshbersin/2014/06/25/quantified-self-meet-the-quantified-employee/#471a6863c5fe.

22. Steven Rosenbaum, "The Quantified Self—Measuring to Curate Your Life," *Forbes*, May 17, 2015, www.forbes.com/sites/stevenrosenbaum/2015/05/17/the-quantified-self-measuring-to-curate-your-life/.

23. Ray Kurzweil and Terry Grossman, *Fantastic Voyage: Live Long Enough to Live Forever* (New York: Rodale, 2004), 34.

24. "Eric Topol," Wikipedia, https://en.wikipedia.org/wiki/Eric_Topol.

25. Olly Bootle, "Gadgets 'Giving Us the Lowdown on Our Health,'" BBC News, August 12, 2013, www.bbc.com/news/health-23619790.

26. David Browne, "The Rise of the Health Coach," *Men's Fitness*, www.mensjournal.com/health-fitness/health/the-rise-of-the-health-coach-20131206.

27. Tony Horton, *Crush It!: Burn Fat, Build Muscle and Shred Inches*

with Ultra-Extreme Warrior's Workout!, digital book, at Amazon. com, www.amazon.com/CRUSH-IT-Ultra-Extreme-Warriors-Workout-ebook/dp/B007UT2A9S.

28.   https://twitter.com/P90X/status/ 642034573803700224?ref_src=twsrc^google |twcamp^ser-p|twgr^tweet.

29.   Heather Havrilesky, "Why Are Americans So Fascinated with Extreme Fitness?," *New York Times Magazine*, October 14, 2014, www.nytimes.com/2014/10/19/magazine/why-are-americans-so-fascinated-with-extreme-fitness.html.

30.   "Zombie Apocalypse Update: October 31, 2015," CrossFit Games, https://games.crossfit.com/video/zombie-apocalypse-up-date- october-31-2015.

31.   Quoted in "Bantu in the Bathroom: Jacqueline Rose on the Trial of Oscar Pistorius," *London Review of Books* 37, no. 22 (November 19, 2015): 3–10, www.lrb.co.uk/v37/n22/jacqueline-rose/bantu-in-the-bathroom.

CHAPTER FIVE: THE MADNESS OF MINDFULNESS

1.   Deepak Chopra, "How to Start Listening to Your Body," Oprah.com, www.oprah.com/spirit/How-to-Start-Listening-to-Your-Body.

2.   Michael Taylor, "What Does 'Listen to Your Body' Actually Mean?," *mindbodygreen*, November 15, 2013, www.mindbodygreen.com/0-11660/what-does-listen-to-your-body-actually-mean.html.

3.   "Manichaeism," Wikipedia, https://en.wikipedia.org/wiki/ Manichaeism.

4.   Quoted in Susan Bordo, *Unbearable Weight: Feminism, Western Culture, and the Body*, 10th anniversary ed. (Berkeley: University of California Press, 2003), 148.

5.   "New Microsoft Study Shows Rapid Decline in Attention Spans," *Mrs. Mindfulness*, http://mrsmindfulness.com/new-microsoft-study-shows-rapid-decline-attention-spans/.

6.   Alan Schwarz, "The Selling of Attention Deficit Disorder," *New York Times*, December 14, 2013, www.nytimes.com/2013/12/15/health/the-selling-of-attention-deficit-disorder.html?pagewanted=all&_r=0.

7. Ibid.

8. Lizette Borreli, "Human Attention Span Shortens to 8 Seconds Due to Digital Technology: 3 Ways to Stay Focused," *Medical Daily*, May 14, 2015, www.medicaldaily.com/human-attention-span-shortens-8-seconds-due-digital-technology-3-ways-stay-focused-333474.

9. Ruth Buczynski, "Do Electronic Devices Affect Sleep?," National Institute for the Clinical Application of Behavioral Medicine, www.nicabm.com/brain-electronics-the-brain-and-sleep54892/.

10. Steve Silberman, "The Geek Syndrome," *Wired*, December 1, 2012, http://archive.wired.com/wired/archive/9.12/aspergers_pr.html.

11. "Silicon Valley syndrome," Urban Dictionary, www.urban dictionary.com/define.php ?term=Silicon+Valley+syndrome.

12. Rebecca Greenfield, "Digital Detox Camp Is So Easy to Hate," *Atlantic*, July 9, 2013, www.theatlantic.com/technology/archive/2013/07/digital-detox-camp-so-easy-hate/313498/.

13. Farhad Manjoo, "Silicon Valley Has an Arrogance Problem," *Wall Street Journal*, November 3, 2013, www.wsj.com/articles/SB10001424052702303661404579175 712015473766.

14. Evgeny Morozov, "The Perils of Perfection," *New York Times*, March 2, 2013, www.nytimes.com/2013/03/03/ opinion/sunday/the-perils-of-perfection.html?_r=0.

15. Liat Clark, "Vinod Khosla: Machines Will Replace 80 Percent of Doctors," *Wired*, September 4, 2012, www.wired.co.uk/news/archive/2012-09/04/doctors-replaced-with-machines.

16. Dave Asprey and J. J. Virgin, *The Bulletproof Diet: Lose Up to a Pound a Day, Reclaim Energy and Focus, Upgrade Your Life* (New York: Rodale, 2014), ebook, location 125.

17. Ray Kurzweil and Terry Grossman, *Fantastic Voyage: Live Long Enough to Live Forever* (New York: Rodale, 2004), 141.

18. Ibid.

19. Betsy Isaacson, "Silicon Valley Is Trying to Make Humans Immortal—And Finding Some Success," *Newsweek*, March 5, 2015, www.newsweek.com/2015/03/13/silicon-valley-trying-make-humans-immortal-and-finding-some-success-311402.html.

20. Jeff Bercovici, "How Peter Thiel Is Trying to Save the World," *Inc.*, July/August 2015, www.inc.com/magazine/201507/jeff-bercovici/can-peter-thiel-save-the-world.html.

21. Line Goguen-Hughes, "Mindfulness and Innovation," *Mindful*, November 9, 2011, www.mindful.org/mindfulness-and-innovation/.

22.   Soren Gordhamer, *Wisdom 2.0: The New Movement Toward Purposeful Engagement in Business and in Life* (New York: HarperOne, 2013), 4.

23.   Katie Hing, "Monk Who Inspired Gwyneth Paltrow and Emma Watson Now Worth £25 Million," *Mirror*, July 4, 2015, www.mirror.co.uk/3am/celebrity-news/monk-who-inspired-gwyneth-paltrow-6003291.

24.   Bill Barol, "The Monk and the Mad Man Making Mindfulness for the Masses," *Fast Company*, January 28, 2015, www.fastcompany.com/3041402/body-week/the-monk-and-the-mad-man-making-mindfulness-for-the-masses.

25.   Erin Anderssen, "Digital Overload: How We Are Seduced by Distraction," *Globe and Mail*, March 29, 2014, www.theglobeandmail.com/life/ relationships/digital-overload-how-we-are-seduced-by-distraction/article17725778/?page=all.

26.   HarperCollins New Zealand promotional page for Soren Gordhamer, *Wisdom 2.0*, www.harpercollins.co.nz/9780061899256/wisdom-2-0.

27.   David Gelles, "The Mind Business," *Financial Times*, August 24, 2012, www.ft.com/intl/cms/s/2/d9cb7940-ebea-11e1-985a-00144feab49a.html#axzz24gGdUpNS.

28.   Marc Kaufman, "Meditation Gives Brain a Charge, Study Finds," *Washington Post*, January 3, 2005, www.washingtonpost.com/wp-dyn/articles/A43006-2005Jan2.html.

29.   http://archinte.jamanetwork.com/article.aspx?articleid=1809754.

30.   I. Plaza, M. M. Demarzo, P. Herrera-Mercadal, and J. García-Campayo, "Mindfulness-Based Mobile Applications: Literature Review and Analysis of Current Features," *Journal of Medical Internet Research mHealth uHealth* 1, no. 2 (November 1, 2013), www.ncbi.nlm.nih.gov/pubmed/25099314.

31.   Jo Confino, "Google's Head of Mindfulness: 'Goodness Is Good for Business,'" *Guardian*, May 14, 2014, www.theguardian.com/sustainable-business/google-meditation-mindfulness-technology.

32.   Emily McManus, "Why Aren't We Asking the Big Questions? A Q&A with Ruby Wax," *TED Blog*, October 10, 2012, http://blog.ted.com/why-arent-we-asking-the-big-questions-a-qa-with-ruby-wax/.

CHAPTER SIX: DEATH IN SOCIAL CONTEXT

1. Susan Dominus, "The Lives They Lived; Ladies of the Gym Unite!," *New York Times Magazine*, December 8, 2003, www.nytimes.com/2003/12/28/magazine/the-lives-they-lived-ladies-of-the-gym-unite.html.

2. Dick Cavett, "When That Guy Died on My Show," *Opinionator* (blog), *New York Times*, May 3, 2007, http://opinionator.blogs.nytimes.com/2007/05/03/when-that-guy-died-on-my-show/?_r=0.

3. Chris Crowley, "Harry Lodge: A Personal Memoir," *Younger Next Year*, March 16, 2017, www.youngernextyear.com/harry-lodge-personal-memoir/.

4. Quoted in Howard M. Leichter, "'Evil Habits' and 'Personal Choices': Assigning Responsibility for Health in the 20th Century," *Milbank Quarterly* 81, no. 4 (December 2003): 603–26, www.ncbi.nlm.nih.gov/pmc/articles/PMC2690243/.

5. Raymond Downing, *Biohealth: Beyond Medicalization: Imposing Health* (Eugene, OR: Wipf and Stock Publishers, 2011).

6. Ian Shapira, "What Kind of Cancer Killed Them? Obituaries for David Bowie and Others Don't Say," *Washington Post*, January 22, 2016, www.washingtonpost.com/local/what-kind-of-cancer-killed-them-eobituaries-for-david-bowie-and-others-dont-say/2016/01/21/b4ac24e8-bf9a-11e5-83d4-42e3bceea902_story.html.

7. Walter Isaacson, *Steve Jobs* (New York: Simon and Schuster, 2011), 224.

8. Mark Molesky, *This Gulf of Fire: The Destruction of Lisbon, Or Apocalypse in the Age of Science and Reason* (New York: Alfred A. Knopf, 2015), 55.

9. "*Poème sur le désastre de Lisbonne*," Wikipedia, https://en.wikipedia.org/wiki/Po%C3%A8me_sur_le_d%C3%A9sastre_de_Lisbonne

10. Quoted in Michael Fitzpatrick, *The Tyranny of Health: Doctors and the Regulation of Lifestyle* (New York: Routledge, 2002), 9.

11. Quoted in ibid.

12. Arun Gupta, "How TV Superchef Jamie Oliver's 'Food Revolution' Flunked Out," *AlterNet*, April 7, 2010, www.alternet.org/story/146354/how_tv_superchef_jamie_oliver's_'food_revolution'_flunked_out.

13. Gary Taubes, "What If It's All Been a Big Fat Lie?," *New York Times Magazine*, July 7, 2002, www.nytimes.com/2002/07/07/

magazine/what-if-it-s-all-been-a-big-fat-lie.html.

14. John Steinbeck, *In Dubious Battle* (1936).

15. "Death of Eric Garner," Wikipedia, https://en.wikipedia.org/wiki/Death_of_Eric_Garner.

16. Christopher Mathias, "I Love 'Loosies': In Defense of Black Market Cigarettes," *Huffington Post*, April 6, 2011, www.huffingtonpost.com/ christopher-mathias/i-love-loosies-in-defense_b_845698.html.

17. Hilary Graham, "Gender and Class as Dimensions of Smoking Behaviour in Britain: Insights from a Survey of Mothers," *Social Science & Medicine* 38 (1994): 691–98.

18. Linda Tirado, "This Is Why Poor People's Bad Decisions Make Perfect Sense," *Huffington Post*, November 22, 2013, www.huffingtonpost.com/ linda-tirado/why-poor-peoples-bad-decisions-make-perfect-sense_b_4326233.html.

19. Aspen Institute Economic Opportunities Program, Working in America, "Retail Workforce, Employment and Job Quality," December 2015, https://assets.aspeninstitute.org/ content/uploads/files/content/upload/Shop%20Til%20Who%20Drops%20-%20Backgrounder%20-%20FINAL.pdf.

20. Gina Kolata, "A Surprising Secret to a Long Life: Stay in School," *New York Times*, January 3, 2007, www.nytimes.com/2007/01/03/health/03aging.html?_r=0.

21. Kimberly Palmer, "Do Rich People Live Longer?," *U.S. News & World Report*, February 14, 2012, http://money.usnews.com/money/personal-finance/articles/2012/02/14/do-rich-people-live-longer.

22. Sabrina Tavernise, "Disparity in Life Spans of the Rich and the Poor Is Growing," *New York Times*, February 12, 2016, www.nytimes.com/2016/02/13/health/disparity-in-life-spans-of-the-rich-and-the-poor-is-growing.html?

23. "Prescription Painkiller Overdoses at Epidemic Levels," CDC Newsroom, November 1, 2011, www.cdc.gov/ media/releases/2011/p1101_flu_pain_killer_overdose.html.

24. Eugen Tomiuc, "Low Life Expectancy Continues to Plague Former Soviet Countries," Radio Free Europe/Radio Liberty, April 2, 2013, www.rferl.org/content/life-expectancy-cis-report/24946030.html.

25. Tom Engelhardt, quoted in Barbara Ehrenreich, *Dancing in the Streets: A History of Collective Joy* (New York: Metropolitan Books, 2006), 161.

26. Ibid., 162.
27. Alex Cohen, "The Mental Health of Indigenous Peoples: An International Overview," *Cultural Survival Quarterly Magazine*, June 1999, www.culturalsurvival.org/ourpublica tions/csq/article/the-mental-health-indigenous-peoples-an-international-overview.
28. G. William Domhoff, "Wealth, Income, and Power," WhoRulesAmerica.net, September 2005, updated April 2017, www2.ucsc.edu/whorulesamerica/power/wealth.html.
29. Judy Peres, "Workplace Wellness Programs Popular, but Do They Improve Health?," *Chicago Tribune*, December 12, 2014, www.chicagotribune.com/news/ct-workplace-wellness-met-20141212-story.html.
30. Absolute Travel, http://absolutetravel.com/special-interest-travel-tours/wellness-retreats/.
31. "Purity of Heart Is to Will One Thing by Sören [*sic*] Kierkegaard," www.religion-online.org/ showbook.asp?title=2523.

CHAPTER SEVEN: THE WAR BETWEEN CONFLICT AND HARMONY

1. Quoted in David Kaiser, *How the Hippies Saved Physics: Science, Counterculture, and the Quantum Revival* (New York: W. W. Norton, 2011), 266.
2. Penny Lewis, *Integrative Holistic Health, Healing, and Transformation: A Guide for Practitioners, Consultants, and Administrators* (Springfield, IL: Charles C. Thomas, 2002), 20.
3. Ibid., 21.
4. "Systems and Systems Thinking," Encyclopedia.com, www.encyclopedia.com/science/encyclopedias-almanacs-transcripts-and-maps/systems-and-systems-thinking.
5. Joel C. Magnuson, "Pathways to a Mindful Economy," *Society and Economy* 29, no. 2 (2007): 253–84, www.jstor.org/stable/41472084?seq=1#page_scan_tab_contents.
6. George Plopper, *Principles of Cell Biology* (Burlington, MA: Jones & Bartlett Learning, 2014).
7. "William Harvey," www.umich.edu/~ece/student_projects/anatomy/ people_pages/harvey.html.
8. George Johnson, *The Cancer Chronicles: Unlocking Medicine's*

Deepest Mystery (New York: Alfred A. Knopf, 2013), 143; Brett Israel, "How Many Cancers Are Caused by the Environment?," *Scientific American* via *Environmental Health News*, May 21, 2010, www.scientificamerican.com/ article/how-many-cancers-are-caused-by-the-environment/.

9. DeLisa Fairweather and Noel R. Rose, "Women and Autoimmune Diseases," *Emerging Infectious Diseases* 10, no. 11 (2004): 2005–11, wwwnc.cdc.gov/eid/article/10/11/04-0367_article.

10. Quoted in Alfred I. Tauber, "Immunology and the Enigma of Selfhood," in *Growing Explanations: Historical Perspective on Recent Science*, ed. M. Norton Wise (Durham, NC: Duke University Press, 2004), 207.

11. Alfred I. Tauber, *The Immune Self: Theory or Metaphor?* (Cambridge: Cambridge University Press, 1994), 141.

12. Quoted in Emily Martin, "Toward an Anthropology of Immunology: The Body as Nation State," *Medical Anthropology Quarterly*, New Series, vol. 4, no. 4 (December 1990): 410–26, quote on 411.

13. Quoted in Warwick Anderson and Ian R. Mackay, *Intolerant Bodies: A Short History of Autoimmunity* (Baltimore: Johns Hopkins University Press, 2014), 89.

14. Lois N. Magner, *A History of Infectious Diseases and the Microbial World* (Healing Society: Disease, Medicine, and History) (Westport, CT: Praeger, 2009), 205.

15. Quoted in Anderson and Mackay, *Intolerant Bodies*, 89.

16. "Talking to Your Child About Menstruation," KidsHealth, http://kidshealth.org/parent/positive/talk/talk_about_menstruation.html#.

17. Karol Maybury, "A Positive Approach to Menarche and Menstruation," Society for the Psychology of Women, American Psychological Association, www.apadivisions.org/division-35/news-events/news/menstruation.aspx.

18. "Margie Profet," Wikipedia, https://en.wikipedia.org/wiki/Margie_Profet.

19. Brendan Maher, "Missing Biologist Surfaces, Reunites with Family," Nature.com, May 31, 2012, http://blogs.nature.com/news/2012/05/missing-biologist-surfaces-reunites-with-family.html.

20. Austin Burt and Robert Trivers, *Genes in Conflict: The Biology of Selfish Genetic Elements* (Cambridge, MA: Harvard University Press, 2006), 3.

21. Suzanne Sadedin, "What Is the Evolutionary Benefit or Purpose of Having Periods?," Quora, updated November 7, 2016, www.quora.com/

What-is-the-evolutionary-benefit-or-purpose-of-having-periods.

CHAPTER EIGHT: CELLULAR TREASON

1.   Ruqaiyyah Siddiqui and Naveed Ahmed Khan, "Acanthamoeba Is
an Evolutionary Ancestor of Macrophages: A Myth or Reality?,"
Experimental Parasitology 130, no. 2 (February 2012): 95–97,
http://ecommons.aku.edu/cgi/viewcontent.cgi?article=
1015&context=pakistan_fhs_mc_bbs.
2.   Emily Martin, "Toward an Anthropology of Immunology: The
Body as Nation State."
3.   Abul K. Abbas, Andrew H. Lichtman, and Shiv Pillai, *Cellular
and Molecular Immunology*, 8th ed. (Philadelphia: Elsevier, 2015),
110–11.
4.   See, for example, David A. Hume, "Macrophages as APC and the
Dendritic Cell Myth," *Journal of Immunology* 181 (2008):
5829–35, www.jimmunol.org/content/181/9/5829.full.pdf.
5.   Quoted in Gary Stix, "A Malignant Flame," *Scientific American*,
July 1, 2008, www.scientificamerican.com/ article/a-malignant-
flame-2008-07/.
6.   Ross Pelton with Lee Overholser, *Alternatives in Cancer Therapy:
The Complete Guide to Non-Traditional Treatments* (New York:
Fireside, 1994), 234.
7.   Jerome Groopman, "The T-Cell Army," *New Yorker*, April 23, 2012,
www.newyorker.com/magazine/2012/04/23/the-t-cell-army.
8.   Toshifumi Fujiwara et al., "Macrophage Infiltration Predicts a
Poor Prognosis for Human Ewing Sarcoma," *American Journal of
Pathology* 179, no. (2011): 1157–70, www.ncbi.nlm.nih.gov/pmc/
articles/PMC3157220/.
9.   Denise Grady, "Harnessing the Immune System to Fight Cancer,"
New York Times, July 30, 2016, www.nytimes.com/2016/07/31/
health/harnessing-the-immune-system-to-fight-cancer.html?_r=0.
10.   John Condeelis and Jeffrey W. Pollard, "Macrophages: Obligate
Partners for Tumor Cell Migration, Invasion, and Metastasis," *Cell*
124, no. 2 (January 2006): 263–66, www.cell.com/cell/ abstract/
S0092-8674%2806%2900055-9.
11.   S. Su et al. "A Positive Feedback Loop Between Mesenchymal-Like
Cancer Cells and Macrophages Is Essential to Breast Cancer Me-

tastasis," *Cancer Cell* 25, no. 5 (May 12, 2014): 605–20, www.ncbi.nlm.nih.gov/pubmed/24823638.

12.   Condeelis and Pollard, "Macrophages: Obligate Partners for Tumor Cell Migration, Invasion, and Metastasis."

13.   "ASCB Celldance 2015 'Spying on Cancer Cell Invasion,'" YouTube, uploaded January 21, 2016, www.youtube.com/watch?v=IvyJKrx5Xmw.

14.   Francis Collins, "Cool Videos: Spying on Cancer Cell Invasion," *NIH Director's Blog*, National Institutes of Health, February 4, 2016, https://directorsblog.nih.gov/2016/02/04/cool-videos-spying-on-cancer-cell-invasion/.

15.   A. Schmall et al., "Macrophage and Cancer Cell Cross-Talk via CCR2 and CX3CR1 Is a Fundamental Mechanism Driving Lung Cancer," *American Journal of Respiratory and Critical Care Medicine* 191, no. 4 (2015): 437–47, www.ncbi.nlm.nih.gov/pubmed/25536148.

16.   Carly Bess Williams, Elizabeth S. Yeh, and Adam C. Soloff, "Tumor-Associated Macrophages: Unwitting Accomplices in Breast Cancer Malignancy," *NPJ Breast Cancer* 2 (2016), www.nature.com/articles/npjb cancer201525.

17.   pHisohex, www.phisohex.com.au/.

18.   Emil A. Tanghetti, "The Role of Inflammation in the Pathology of Acne," *Journal of Clinical and Aesthetic Dermatology* 6, no. 9 (2013): 27–35, www.ncbi.nlm.nih.gov/pmc/articles/PMC3780801/.

19.   Jerome Groopman, "Inflamed: The Debate over the Latest Cure-All Craze," *New Yorker*, November 30, 2015, www.newyorker.com/magazine/2015/11/30/inflamed.

20.   Ibid.

21.   Ira Tabas and Karin E. Bornfeldt, "Macrophage Phenotype and Function in Different Stages of Atherosclerosis," *Circulation Research* 118 (2016): 653–67, http://circres.ahajournals.org/content/118/4/653.abstract.

22.   Groopman, "Inflamed."

23.   "Should You Buy Into an Anti-inflammatory Diet?," Conscien-Health, http://conscienhealth.org/2015/06/should-you-buy-into-anti-inflammatory-diet/.

24.   David M. Mosser and Justin P. Edward, "Exploring the Full Spectrum of Macrophage Activation," *Nature Reviews Immunology* 8, no. 12 (December 2008): 958–69, www.ncbi.nlm.nih.gov/pmc/articles/PMC2724991/.

25. Fabrice Merien, "A Journey with Elie Metchnikoff: From Innate Cell Mechanisms in Infectious Diseases to Quantum Biology," *Frontiers in Public Health* 4 (2016): 125, www.ncbi.nlm.nih.gov/pmc/articles/PMC4909730/.

26. Mosser and Edward, "Exploring the Full Spectrum of Macrophage Activation."

27. Simon Hallam et al., "Activated Macrophages in the Tumour Microenvironment—Dancing to the Tune of TLR and NF-κB," *Journal of Pathology* 219, no. 2 (2009): 143–52, www.ncbi.nlm.nih.gov/pmc/articles/PMC2935674/.

CHAPTER NINE: TINY MINDS

1. Paul de Kruif, *Microbe Hunters* (New York: Harvest, 1996; originally published 1926), 201.

2. Alfred I. Tauber, *The Immune Self: Theory or Metaphor?* (Cambridge: Cambridge University Press, 1994), 19.

3. Ibid., 26.

4. G. Balázsi, A. van Oudenaarden, and J. J. Collins, "Cellular Decision Making and Biological Noise: From Microbes to Mammals," *Cell* 144, no. 6 (2011): 910–25, www.ncbi.nlm.nih.gov/pubmed/21414483.

5. H. Parsa, R. Upadhyay, and S. K. Sia, "Uncovering the Behaviors of Individual Cells Within a Multicellular Microvascular Community," *Proceedings of the National Academy of Sciences* 108, no. 12 (2011): 5133–38, www.ncbi.nlm.nih.gov/pubmed/21383144.

6. Emily Singer, "Evolution of an Individual's Cancer Can Be Tracked Cell by Cell," *Quanta* magazine via *Scientific American*, November 15, 2013, www.scientificamerican.com/article.cfm?id=evolution-of-an-individuals-can-be-tracked-cell-by-cell.

7. Jamie A. Lopez et al., "Rapid and Unidirectional Perforin Pore Delivery at the Cytotoxic Immune Synapse," *Journal of Immunology* 191, no. 5 (2013): 2328–34, www.jimmunol.org/content/191/5/2328.

8. Sindy H. Wei, Ian Parker, Mark J. Miller, and Michael D. Cahalan, "A Stochastic View of Lymphocyte Motility and Trafficking Within the Lymph Node," *Immunological Reviews* 195 (2003): 136–59, http://parkerlab.bio.uci.edu/ publication%20attachments/Wei_ImmRev2003_119.pdf.

9. "Coturnix," "And Now the Scientists Will Do Whatever They

Damned Please (Start Shouting, Most Likely)," *ScienceBlogs*, May 15, 2007, http://scienceblogs.com/clock/2007/05/15/and-now-the-scientists-will-do/.

10.   Bob Holmes, "Fruit Flies Display Rudimentary Free Will," *New Scientist*, May 16, 2007, www.newscientist.com/article/dn11858-fruit-flies-display-rudimentary-free-will/.

11.   Lanying Zeng et al., "Decision Making at a Subcellular Level Determines the Outcome of Bacteriophage Infection," *Cell* 141, no. 4 (2010): 682–91, www.ncbi.nlm.nih.gov/pmc/articles/PMC2873970/.

12.   "Freeman J. Dyson Interview," *Think Atheist*, April 5, 2010, www.thinkatheist.com/group/thinkingape/forum/topics/freeman-j-dyson-interview.

13.   Jessica Riskin, *The Restless Clock: A History of the Centuries-Long Argument over What Makes Things Tick* (Chicago: University of Chicago Press, 2016), 3.

14.   Ibid.

15.   Carolyn Merchant, *The Death of Nature: Women, Ecology, and the Scientific Revolution* (New York: HarperCollins, 1982).

CHAPTER TEN: "SUCCESSFUL AGING"

1.   Chris Crowley and Henry S. Lodge, *Younger Next Year: Live Strong, Fit, and Sexy—Until You're 80 and Beyond* (New York: Workman, 2004), 49.

2.   Ibid., 111.

3.   "Jeanne Calment," Wikipedia, https://en.wikipedia.org/wiki/Jeanne_Calment.

4.   Sarah Lamb et al., *Successful Aging as a Contemporary Obsession: Global Perspectives*. (New Brunswick, NJ: Rutgers University Press, 2017).

5.   *The Gerontologist* published its February 2015 edition as a "Special Issue on Successful Aging," reflecting on the concept's past and future. Beyond gerontology proper, see also the Spring 2015 issue of *Daedalus: Journal of the American Academy of the Arts and Sciences*, dedicated to the "Successful Aging of Societies." See also John W. Rowe and Robert L. Kahn, "Successful Aging 2.0: Conceptual Expansions for the 21st Century," *Journals of Gerontology, Series B: Psychological Sciences and Social Sciences* 70, no. 4 (2015): 593-96.

6. The full name of this conference was "European Year for Active
    Aging and Solidarity Between Generations." See
    http://ec.europa.eu/archives/ey2012/.

7. Sarah Lamb, "Permanent Personhood or Meaningful Decline?
    Toward a Critical Anthropology of Successful Aging," *Journal of Aging
    Studies* 29 (2014): 41–52, https://medschool.vanderbilt.edu/
    psychiatry-geriatric-fellowship/files/psychiatry-geriatric-fellowship/
    public_files/Aging%20-%20 meaningful%20decline.pdf.

8. Crowley and Lodge, *Younger Next Year*, 29.

9. Richard Conniff, "The Hunger Gains: Extreme Calorie-Restriction
    Diet Shows Anti-Aging Results," *Scientific American*, February 16,
    2016, www.scientificamerican.com/article/the-hunger-gains-extreme-
    calorie-restriction-diet-shows-anti-aging-results/.

10. Roger Landry, "The Person Who Will Live to Be 150 Is Alive
    Today—Could He Be You?," *U.S. News & World Report*, August
    19, 2015, via Yahoo News, www.yahoo.com/news/person-
    live-150-alive-today-could-110000115.html?ref=gs.

11. Quoted in Lynne Segal, *Out of Time: The Pleasures and the Perils of
    Ageing* (New York: Verso, 2014), 178.

12. Deirdre Carmody, "At Lunch With: Betty Friedan; Trying to Dispel
    'The Mystique of Age' at 72," *New York Times*, September 15, 1993,
    www.nytimes.com/books/99/05/09/specials/friedan-lunch.html.

13. U.S. Census Bureau, "Mobility Is Most Common Disability
    Among Older Americans, Census Bureau Reports," press release,
    December 2, 2014, www.census.gov/newsroom/press-releases/
    2014/cb14-218.html.

14. Stewart Green, "Death on Mount Everest," ThoughtCo., March 2,
    2017, www.thoughtco.com/death-on-mount-everest-755907.

15. See, for example, International Mountain Guides,
    www.mountainguides.com/everest-south.shtml.

16. Paula Span, "High Disability Rates Persist in Old Age," *New York
    Times*, July 8, 2013, http://newoldage.blogs.nytimes.com/2013/
    07/08/high-disability- rates-persist-in-old-age/?_r=0.

17. Cavan Sieczkowski, "Blake Lively Announces Lifestyle Company
    Similar to Gwyneth Paltrow's GOOP," *Huffington Post*, September
    26, 2013, www.huffingtonpost.com/2013/09/26/blake-lively-
    lifestyle-company_n_3997565.html.

18. Molly Young, "How Amanda Chantal Bacon Perfected the
    Celebrity Wellness Business," *New York Times Magazine*, May 25,
    2017, www.nytimes.com/2017/05/25/magazine/how-amanda-
    chantal-bacon-perfected-the-celebrity-wellness-business.html.

19. "The Importance of Touch for Seniors," *The Arbors Blog*, March 23, 2017, http://blog.arborsassistedliving.com/importance-of-touch-for-seniors.

20. Siyi Chen, "Intimacy for Rent: Inside the Business of Paid Cuddling," *Quartz*, October 6, 2016, https://qz.com/779547/intimacy-for-rent-inside-the-business-of-paid-cuddling/.

21. Martha Savaria Morris, "The Role of B Vitamins in Preventing and Treating Cognitive Impairment and Decline," *Advances in Nutrition* 3 (2012): 801–12, http://advances.nutrition.org/content/3/6/801.full.

22. Katarzyna Szarc vel Szic, Ken Declerck, Melita Vidaković, and Wim Vanden Berghe, "From Inflammaging to Healthy Aging by Dietary Lifestyle Choices: Is Epigenetics the Key to Personalized Nutrition?," *Clinical Epigenetics* 7, no. 1 (2015): 33, www.ncbi.nlm.nih.gov/pmc/articles/PMC4389409/.

23. "Blocking Brain Inflammation 'Halts Alzheimer's Disease,'" BBC News, January 8, 2016, www.bbc.com/news/health-35254649.

24. Philip Roth, *Everyman* (Boston: Houghton Mifflin Harcourt, 2006), 155.

25. Kathryn Higgins, "The Immune Cell, the Neutrophil—The Good, the Bad, or the Ugly?," *Brainwaves*, February 21, 2012, www.sciencebrainwaves.com/the-immune-cell-the-neutrophil-the-good-the-bad-or-the-ugly/.

26. Alfred I. Tauber, *The Immune Self*, 8.

27. Quoted in Mary Roach, *Stiff: The Curious Lives of Human Cadavers* (New York: W. W. Norton, 2003), 68.

CHAPTER ELEVEN: THE INVENTION OF THE SELF

1. Henry Wadsworth Longfellow, "A Psalm of Life," Poetry Foundation, www.poetryfoundation.org/poems-and-poets/poems/detail/44644.

2. Gary Petty, "What Does the Bible Say About the 'Immortal Soul,'" *Beyond Today*, July 15, 1999, www.ucg.org/the-good-news/what-does-the-bible-say-about-the-immortal-soul.

3. Lionel Trilling, *Sincerity and Authenticity* (Cambridge, MA: Harvard University Press, 1973), 19.

4. Jean-Jacques Rousseau, *The Confessions and Correspondence, Including the Letters to Malesherbes*, trans. Christopher Kelly (Hanover, NH: University Press of New England, 1995), ebook, location 693.

5.   John O. Lyons, *The Invention of the Self: The Hinge of Consciousness in the Eighteenth Century* (Carbondale: Southern Illinois University Press, 1978).

6.   "Martin Guerre," Wikipedia, https://en.wikipedia.org/wiki/Martin_Guerre.

7.   Garth Amundson, "Psychotherapy, Religion, and the Invention of the Self," *Therapy View: Musings on the Work and Play of Psychotherapy*, November 1, 2015, https://therapyviews.com/2015/11/01/do-psychiatric-drugs-offer-a-meaningful-resolution-of-human-suffering/.

8.   Marino Perez-Alvarez, "Hyperreflexivity as a Condition of Mental Disorder: A Clinical and Historical Perspective," *Psicothema* 20, no. 2 (2008): 181–87.

9.   "Worshiping Yourself," *The Twisted Rope*, March 6, 2014, https://thetwistedrope.wordpress.com/2014/03/06/worshiping-yourself/.

10. Barbara Ehrenreich, *Dancing in the Streets: A History of Collective Joy* (New York: Metropolitan Books, 2006).

11. Herbert Fingarette, *Death: Philosophical Soundings* (Chicago: Open Court, 1999), 34–35.

12. Alex Lickerman, "Overcoming the Fear of Death," *Psychology Today*, October 8, 2009, www.psychologytoday.com/blog/happiness-in-world/200910/overcoming-the-fear-death.

13. Robert C. Solomon, *Spirituality for the Skeptic: The Thoughtful Love of Life* (Oxford: Oxford University Press, 2006), 120.

14. Amundson, "Psychotherapy, Religion, and the Invention of the Self."

15. Noah Shachtman, "Troops Use 'Samurai' Meditation to Soothe PTSD," *Wired*, October 8, 2008, www.wired.com/2008/10/samurai-soldier/.

16. "Rupert Brooke's Obituary in *The Times*," http://exhibits.lib.byu.edu/wwi/poets/rbobituary.html.

17. "Joe Hill," Union Songs, http://unionsong.com/u017.html.

18. Daniel Goleman, "The Experience of Touch: Research Points of a Critical Role," *New York Times*, February 2, 1988, www.nytimes.com/1988/02/02/science/the-experience-of-touch-research-points-to-a-critical-role.html?pagewanted=all.

19. Robinson Meyer, "Human Extinction Isn't That Unlikely," *Atlantic*, April 29, 2016, www.theatlantic.com/technology/archive/2016/04/a-human-extinction-isnt-that-unlikely/480444/.

20. "The Irreconcilable Acceptance of Near-Term Extinction," *Nature Bats Last*, April 28, 2013, https://guymcpherson.com/2013/04/the-irreconcilable-acceptance-of-near-term-extinction/.

CHAPTER TWELVE: KILLING THE SELF, REJOICING IN A LIVING WORLD

1. "Jacques Monod," Today in Science History,
    https://todayinsci.com/M/Monod_Jacques/MonodJacques-
    Quotations.htm.
2. "The Triumph of Abrahamic Monotheism?," *Religion Today*,
    November 2, 2011, http://religion-today.blogspot.com/2011/11/
    triumph-of-abrahamic-monotheism.html.
3. Jessica Riskin, *The Restless Clock: A History of the Centuries-Long
    Argument over What Makes Things Tick* (Chicago: University of
    Chicago Press, 2016), 3.
4. Jackson Lears, "Material Issue," *The Baffler*, no. 32 (September
    2016), https://thebaffler.com/salvos/material-issue-lears.
5. George Dvorsky, "Prominent Scientists Sign Declaration That Ani-
    mals Have Conscious Awareness, Just Like Us," Gizmodo, August 23,
    2012, http://io9.gizmodo.com/5937356/prominent-scientists-sign-
    declaration-that-animals-have-conscious-awareness-just-like-us.
6. Stephen Hawking, "The Origin of the Universe," Hawking.org.uk,
    www.hawking.org.uk/the-origin-of-the-universe.html.
7. Rolf Ent, Thomas Ullrich, and Raju Venugopalan, "The Glue That
    Binds Us," *Scientific American*, May 2015, www.bnl.gov/physics/
    NTG/link able_files/pdf/SciAm-Glue-Final.pdf.
8. David Rieff, *Swimming in a Sea of Death: A Son's Memoir* (New
    York, Simon & Schuster, 2008), 167.
9. Ibid.
10. Michael Pollan, "The Trip Treatment," *New Yorker*, February 9,
    2015, www.newyorker.com/magazine/2015/02/09/trip-treatment.
11. Ibid.
12. Ibid.
13. Simon G. Powell, *Magic Mushroom Explorer: Psilocybin and the
    Awakening Earth* (South Paris, ME: Park Street Press, 2015), 30.
14. Pollan, "The Trip Treatment."
15. "Bertolt Brecht: When in My White Room at the Charité," repro-
    duced at *Tom Clark Beyond the Pale*, January 12, 2012,
    http://tomclarkblog.blogspot.com/2012/01/bertolt-brecht-
    when-in-my-white-room-at.html.

INDEX

Also by Barbara Ehrenreich and available from Granta Books

www.granta.com

Global Woman

Nannies, Maids and Sex Workers
in the New Economy

Also by Barbara Ehrenreich and available from Granta Books

www.granta.com

Blood Rites

The Origins and History
of the Passions of War

'One of those rare books that make you question
everything you thought you knew' Susan Faludi

What lies behind the human attraction to violence? Why do we
glorify war, seeing it as an almost sacred undertaking? Known for
the originality of her thinking, Barbara Ehrenreich proposes a radical theory about our attitudes to bloodshed. From the trenches of
Verdun to today's front lines, she traces the history of warfare all
the way back to our prehistoric ancestors' terrifying experiences of
being hunted by other carnivores. Written with wit, tenacity and
intellectual flair, *Blood Rites* will transform our understanding of
human conflict.

'An extraordinary book, original and
witty . . . shocking and gripping' *Irish Times*

'Keen and arresting . . . One of today's most
original writers has tackled one of humankind's
most intractable subjects' *New York Times*

'Revealing, provocative and fascinating' *The Times*

Nickel and Dimed

Undercover in Low-Wage USA

'By anyone's standards, *Nickel and Dimed* is an extraordinary achievement . . . Ehrenreich has produced what is surely one of the most gripping political books ever written' *Observer*

'An extraordinary Orwellian testimony to how tough American working life is for the bottom 20 per cent' Will Hutton

'Ehrenreich's deceptively upbeat and personal style, carefully barbed in all the right places, packs shocking economic statistics into footnotes . . . That's what *Nickel and Dimed* is really about – the act of making the invisible visible, a crucial and timely act. Read it' Ali Smith, *Scotsman*

'This is an unputdownable book, excellent journalism researched "hands-on" in the old-fashioned way . . . should be obligatory reading for all government departments dealing with low-paid workers . . . an excellent book, a great read' *Irish Independent*

'As a straight-ahead political intervention the book is admirable and important, but it is also far more than that . . . this book is ultimately about the kinds of relationships we have with other human beings . . . it's a message that should be heeded and a book that must be read' *Independent on Sunday*

Also by Barbara Ehrenreich and available from Granta Books

www.granta.com

Bait and Switch

The Futile Pursuit
of the Corporate Dream

'A compelling exploration of the human cost of the flexible
labour market and the culture of shareholder value that
have become the hallmarks of modern business, not only
in the US but increasingly in Europe' *Irish Times*

'This is a very funny book, and a briskly humane
one' *Times Literary Supplement*

'A wonderful, depressing look at the grim netherworld of
unemployment in what is rather optimistically referred to as
America's corporate executive class, and the psycho-babbling
"career coaches" who leech off the despair' *Guardian*

'Ehrenreich is brilliant at highlighting the darkest corners
of the corporate world which are the driving forces behind
middle-class poverty, personal crises, breadowns in family
structures, stress and depression . . . a wonderful and
daring exposé and an overdue warning about the shape of
things to come for the white-collar workforce' *Tribune*

'Ehrenreich is once again a smart, mordant observer . . . great,
acerbic company for the reader' *Scotsman*

Also by Barbara Ehrenreich and available from Granta Books

www.granta.com

Dancing in the Streets

A History of Collective Joy

'An admirably lucid, level-headed history of outbreaks
of collective joy from Dionysus to the Grateful
Dead . . . full of fascinating vignettes' Terry Eagleton

'This is a passionate argument in favour of communal
celebration . . . Ehrenreich tackles this question with brio, offering
an ambitious account of cultural history . . . This book opens
an important subject to the general reader' *Sunday Times*

'Ehrenreich has an ability to write as though she has lived through
the history she relates. Her fascination with how our past affects
our present and future sings from every page' *Daily Telegraph*

'A magnificent scholarly polemic . . . to read someone
who can write so well, has read so much and has so
much to say is a joy indeed' *Independent on Sunday*

'What this timely book forcefully shows is that we are
social beings with a potential for collective activity that
is not always destructive or docile but may be powerfully
restorative. With the world political scene in crisis and the
planet profoundly in need of our remedial help, it is a message
to be welcomed, pondered – and enjoyed' *The Times*

Also by Barbara Ehrenreich and available from Granta Books

www.granta.com

Smile Or Die

How Positive Thinking
Fooled America and the World

'Fascinating, often very funny, and wholly
convincing . . . stunningly good' *Sunday Times*

A frontal attack on the cult of positive thinking from America's
sharpest, smartest commentator, *Smile or Die* is essential reading for anyone who wants to understand how critical thinking has
become marginalised in the US. From health and academia, the
economy to Iraq, Ehrenreich exposes a trail of denial, delusion and
bad faith, and reveals the often disastrous consequences of putting
on 'a happy face'.

'Ehrenreich puts the glazed perkiness of have-a-nice-day culture
on the chopping block. An uplifting read for anyone who resents
being told to "turn that frown upside down"' *The Times*

'Every so often a book appears that so chimes with your
own thinking, yet flies so spectacularly in the face of
fashionable philosophy, that it comes as a profoundly
reassuring relief' Jenni Murray, *Observer*

'Beguilingly sharp, witty and clear-eyed . . . Ehrenreich
throughout is bracingly acidic and engaging, but also,
shall we say, surprisingly "un-negative" in the face of
so much smiley-faced idiocy' *Daily Telegraph*

'An invigoratingly aggressive and lucidly intelligent attack on
the multi-tentacled nonsense monster . . . for all the pleasure
to be taken in its acidic wit, *Smile or Die* is deadly serious at its
core . . . Fine, funny and angry' *Daily Mail* 'Book of the Week'

Also by Barbara Ehrenreich and available from Granta Books

www.granta.com

Living with a Wild God

A Non-Believer's Search
for the Truth about Everything

'Fascinating and deeply moving' *Sunday Times*

'Ehrenreich writes like a dream . . . [She] has produced a minor miracle: a book about moments of transcendence that many have experienced but most have privately filed away' *Daily Telegraph*

Acclaimed social critic Barbara Ehrenreich is renowned for her trenchant, witty polemics, her incisive journalism, and her rationalist's unwavering gaze. But during her tumultuous adolescence she experienced an event so strange that she didn't dare write or speak about it – it was the kind of event that other people called a 'mystical experience', and to a steadfast atheist and rationalist, it was nothing less than shattering. Here, Ehrenreich attempts to reconcile this defining moment with her secular understanding of the world. In doing so, she challenges us all to reassess our perceptions of what it means to be alive.

'Exhilarating . . . A fascinating spiritual odyssey, rigorously honest and deeply moving' *Sunday Times*

'[This book] provides not just a vivid subjective account of an intense spiritual experience but an insight into this complex and intriguing woman and writer' *Irish Times*

'Audacious . . . a winning approach to autobiography' *Financial Times*

'Compelling' *Independent*